QUILTING
In No Time

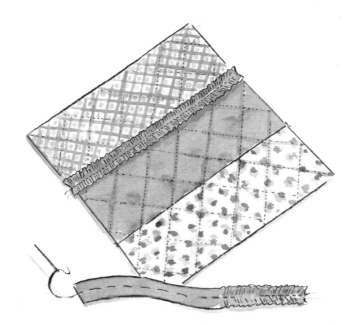

QUILTING
In No Time

50 step-by-step weekend projects made easy

Emma Hardy

CICO BOOKS

LONDON NEW YORK

Published in 2009 by CICO Books
an imprint of Ryland Peters & Small
20–21 Jockey's Fields, London WC1R 4BW

www.cicobooks.co.uk

10 9 8 7 6 5 4 3 2 1

Text copyright © Emma Hardy 2009
Design and photography copyright © CICO Books 2009

A CIP catalogue record for this book is available from the British Library.

ISBN-13: 978 1 906525 29 3

Printed in China

Editor: Marie Clayton
Designer: Liz Sephton
Photographer: Debbie Patterson
Illustrator: Michael Hill

Contents

Introduction

Patchwork and quilting have long been used as a way of creating home furnishings and clothing from scraps of fabric. In the 1800s European immigrants took their skills to America, where they were embraced by the early settlers, as an economical way of producing items from old materials. The craft however can be traced back much further than this with the earliest examples dating back several thousand years.

In more recent times, quilting and patchwork have become an art form as well as a practical craft and there has been a huge resurgence in the last 50 years. Often thought of as slightly old-fashioned, the craft has been taken up by younger, more design-aware crafters who are taking the traditions of quilting and using them in a more contemporary way.

With such an extensive range of fabrics available to us, we no longer have to 'make do' with leftover scraps of fabric, and projects can be designed with specific fabrics in mind incorporating beautiful patterns and colours with stunning results. However, making something from scraps, using leftover pieces of favourite fabrics and eking out small pieces of expensive cloth to create something beautiful is a deeply satisfying process and in our environmentally aware times, can be a great way to recycle and reuse.

In this book I have put together 50 projects ranging from simple coasters that can be made in less than an hour to larger cushions and quilts that take slightly longer to make but none requiring more than a couple of days to complete. With the emphasis on simplicity and style, the projects are designed to be suitable for the novice stitcher as well as the long-time crafter and will fit into all areas of your home, with lots of ideas that would make great gifts, too. Beautifully illustrated, easy-to-follow, step-by-step instructions will lead you confidently through each project and a handy techniques section explains some basic skills with tips on cutting out, piecing and stitching. The projects in this book are all relatively quick to make and include a guide to the amount of time required to complete each one, presuming that you have some sewing experience. Add a little extra time if you are new to needlework.

One of the wonderful things about patchwork and quilting is that there are no limits to the number of original and beautiful results possible. With this in mind, I hope you will be inspired to create many wonderful patchwork projects of your own using and adapting the ideas in this book.

CHAPTER 1

Relaxation Spaces

Sofa Throw

Created from staggered rectangles of fabrics in shades of green and brown, this stylish sofa throw is surprisingly easy to make. As with many quilts, it takes longer to cut out the patchwork pieces than it takes to stitch them together. Speed up the process by using a rotary cutter (see the techniques section) so that several layers of fabric can be cut at the same time. This quilt is backed with fine linen, which drapes beautifully and is hard wearing.

MATERIALS

Enough fabric to make 64 rectangles measuring
15 x 21cm (6 x 8in)

200cm (79in) by the full fabric width of plain natural linen

170 x 130cm (67 x 51in) of cotton wadding

5 buttons

6 hours

1. Cut a paper pattern rectangle measuring 15 x 21cm (6 x 8in). Use this to cut out 64 fabric rectangles in various fabrics. Lay them on the work surface in a row of eight lengthways and with right sides together, pin and stitch them together along the short sides, using a 2cm (⅞in) seam. Press the seams open. Repeat using the remaining fabric rectangles to create eight strips of eight rectangles.

2. With right sides together, pin and stitch these strips together, staggering the seams so that each vertical seam of a new strip falls exactly in the middle of a rectangle on the previous strip. Continue in this way to join all the strips together. Press the seams open and trim the protruding ends of the strips to form a neat panel of patchwork that measures 106 x 143.5cm (41⅞ x 53⅞in).

3. Measure and cut two strips of linen 106 x 7cm (42 x 2¾in). With right sides together, pin and stitch one strip along one end of the patchwork panel (the end being the side with the shorter widths of rectangles). Repeat at the other end with the second strip of linen. Cut two more strips of linen 153.5cm x 7cm (61 x 2¾in). With right sides together, pin and stitch along both sides of the patchwork and press the seams open.

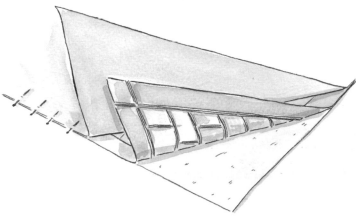

4. Measure and cut a piece of wadding and a piece of linen 153.5 x 116cm (61 x 47in). Lay the patchwork panel wrong side down onto the wadding, smoothing out the layers to make sure that they are completely flat. Lay the linen fabric over the patchwork and pin and stitch through all the layers all the way round, leaving an opening of about 30cm (12in) along one edge. Snip the corners and turn the throw the right way out. Hand stitch the opening and press the whole throw. Sew buttons randomly onto the throw, stitching through all layers to join them.

Log Cabin Cushion Cover

This is a very traditional patchwork, which takes its name from the log cabins built by the early American pioneers. The central panel was traditionally red, representing the hearth, with the surrounding strips, which are all slightly longer than the preceding one, forming the logs around it. I have used a selection of red fabrics here, which all complement each other nicely. Experiment with fabrics in lighter and darker tones for a different effect.

MATERIALS

Scraps of fabric 10cm (4in) wide by the width of the fabric
50 x 80cm (19¾ x 32in) piece of fabric for the back of the cover
45cm (18in) square cushion pad

2 hours

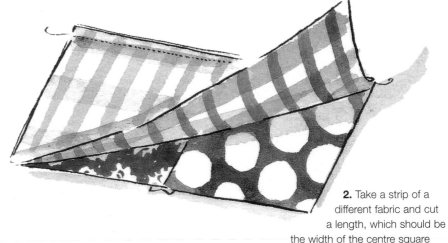

1. Measure and cut a 7cm (2¾in) square of one of the fabrics. Make strips of your fabrics 6cm (2½in) wide by the width of the fabric. The best way to do this is to make a small snip at the edge of the fabric 6cm (2½in) from the edge and tear from the snip. Press all the strips. Cut a piece of one of the strips 7cm (2¾in) long and with right sides together, pin and stitch it to one side of the fabric square. Press the seam open.

2. Take a strip of a different fabric and cut a length, which should be the width of the centre square plus the width of the first strip. With right sides together, pin and stitch this strip in place. Press the seam open.

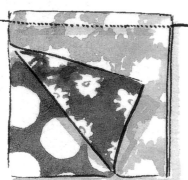

3. Using a strip of fabric in another design, cut a strip for the next side as before and pin and stitch it to the main patchwork panel with right sides together. Press the seam open.

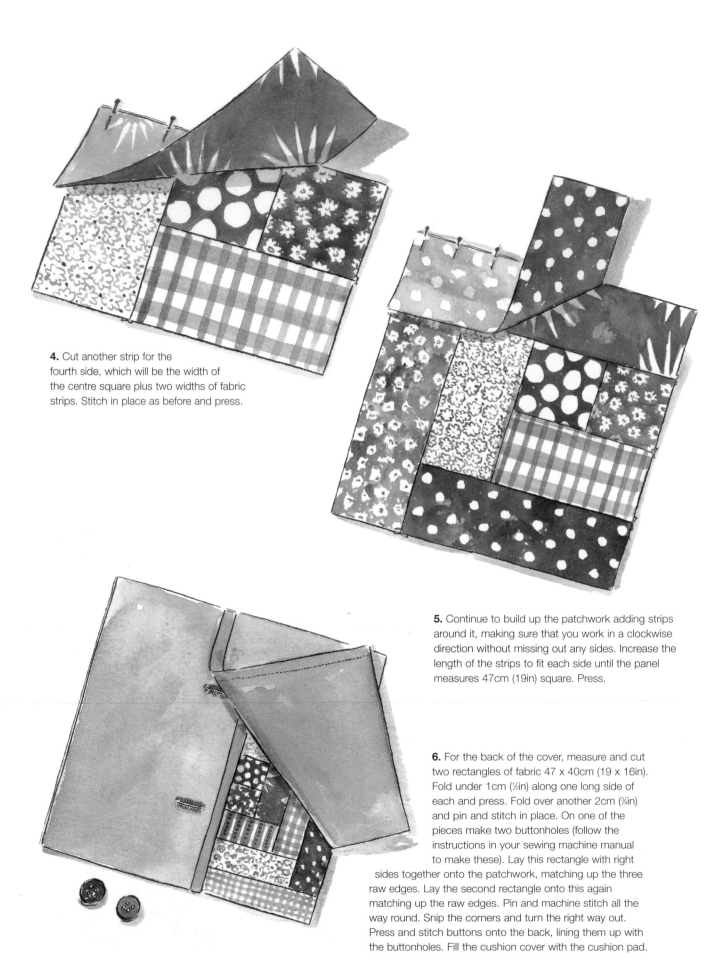

4. Cut another strip for the fourth side, which will be the width of the centre square plus two widths of fabric strips. Stitch in place as before and press.

5. Continue to build up the patchwork adding strips around it, making sure that you work in a clockwise direction without missing out any sides. Increase the length of the strips to fit each side until the panel measures 47cm (19in) square. Press.

6. For the back of the cover, measure and cut two rectangles of fabric 47 x 40cm (19 x 16in). Fold under 1cm (½in) along one long side of each and press. Fold over another 2cm (¾in) and pin and stitch in place. On one of the pieces make two buttonholes (follow the instructions in your sewing machine manual to make these). Lay this rectangle with right sides together onto the patchwork, matching up the three raw edges. Lay the second rectangle onto this again matching up the raw edges. Pin and machine stitch all the way round. Snip the corners and turn the right way out. Press and stitch buttons onto the back, lining them up with the buttonholes. Fill the cushion cover with the cushion pad.

Three Panel Patch Cushion

This patchwork is called rail fence and is made up of blocks of three bars of fabric, which are joined in a nine-patch block. I have used fabrics of a similar colour and tone for a random patchwork, but it can be made with three different coloured fabrics, which can form an attractive zigzag pattern. As with lots of the projects that are made from square blocks joined together, just add more blocks to form a larger patchwork panel to fit a larger cushion – or even make into a quilt.

2 hours

MATERIALS

25 x 90cm (10 x 36in) of each of three different fabrics for the patchwork

Paper for the pattern

60 x 80cm (24 x 32in) piece of fabric for the backing

55cm (22in) square cushion pad

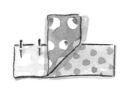

1. Draw and cut a rectangle of paper 20 x 8cm (8 x 3in) to make a paper pattern. Using the paper pattern cut out nine rectangles of each of the three fabrics, so you have 27 in total. With right sides together, pin and stitch one rectangle of each fabric together along the longest sides. Vary the order of the fabrics so that the overall patchwork will be random.

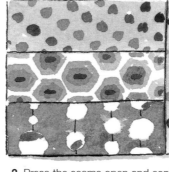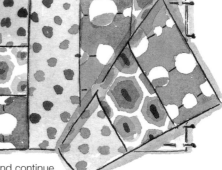

2. Press the seams open and continue to create nine patchwork squares, each made of three rectangles. With right sides together, pin and stitch three of the squares together to form a strip. Arrange them with the bars horizontally, then vertically and the third square horizontally again. Repeat this with the next three squares, laying the bars vertically this time and then horizontally and the last square vertically. Use the last three squares to create a strip like the first one. Press the seams open.

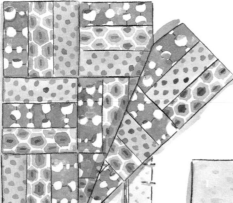

3. With right sides together, pin and stitch the three strips together in their correct order to create the front of the cushion cover. Press the seams open.

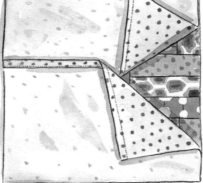

4. To make the back of the cushion cover, cut two rectangles of fabric measuring 56 x 40cm (23 x 16in). Fold over 1cm (½in) along one long side of each piece and again by another 3cm (1¼in). Pin and stitch close to the first fold on both pieces. Lay the patchwork panel right side up on the work surface and lay one of the back pieces onto it with right sides together, lining up the raw edges. Place the second back piece onto the patchwork panel, again lining up the raw edges, so that the hemmed edges overlap each other. Pin and stitch all the way round. Snip the corners off and turn the right way out. Press. Fill the cushion cover with the cushion pad.

Bolster

A bolster adds an interesting decorative touch to a sofa, as well as adding an extra degree of comfort. This bolster cover is made by joining strips of fabric to form a panel, which is then stitched to cover the cushion. This design means that there is no need to sew a zip or buttons and buttonholes onto the cover, because the simple drawstring ends make it simple to fill with the cushion pad and remove it to clean.

1½ hours

MATERIALS

45 x 17cm (18 x 7in) bolster cushion

45 x 60cm (18 x 24in) piece of main fabric

10 x 60cm (4 x 24in) each of three more co-ordinating fabrics

Fabric for piping

120cm (48in) length of piping cord

110cm (44in) length of ribbon

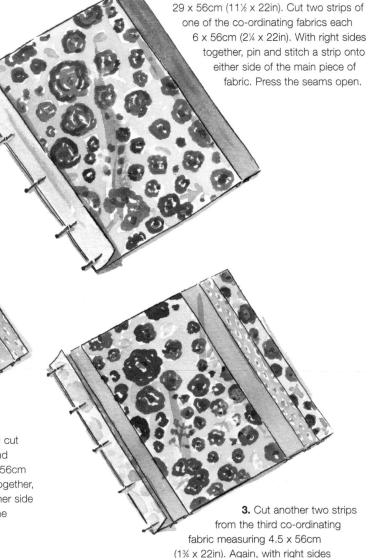

1. Measure and cut a piece of main fabric 29 x 56cm (11½ x 22in). Cut two strips of one of the co-ordinating fabrics each 6 x 56cm (2¼ x 22in). With right sides together, pin and stitch a strip onto either side of the main piece of fabric. Press the seams open.

2. Measure and cut two strips of a second co-ordinating fabric 4.5 x 56cm (1¾ x 22in). With right sides together, pin and stitch a strip onto either side of the main panel, pressing the seams open again.

3. Cut another two strips from the third co-ordinating fabric measuring 4.5 x 56cm (1¾ x 22in). Again, with right sides together, pin and stitch a strip onto either side of the main panel and press the seams open.

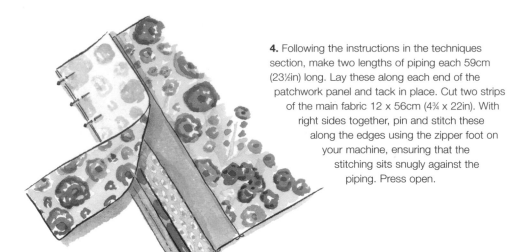

4. Following the instructions in the techniques section, make two lengths of piping each 59cm (23½in) long. Lay these along each end of the patchwork panel and tack in place. Cut two strips of the main fabric 12 x 56cm (4¾ x 22in). With right sides together, pin and stitch these along the edges using the zipper foot on your machine, ensuring that the stitching sits snugly against the piping. Press open.

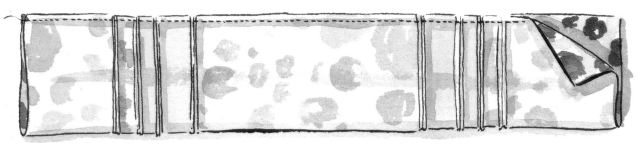

5. Fold the patchwork panel in half with right sides together and pin and stitch along the longest side.

6. Fold under 1cm (½in) to the wrong side at each end of the tube and press. Fold over by another 1cm (½in) and pin and slip stitch in place, leaving a gap of about 1.5cm (⅝in) in the stitching.

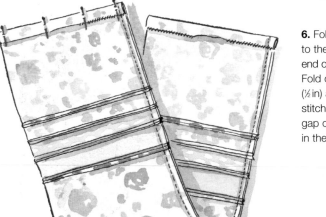

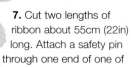

7. Cut two lengths of ribbon about 55cm (22in) long. Attach a safety pin through one end of one of the ribbons and push it through the channel at the end of the fabric tube until it comes back out through the hole. Remove the safety pin and pull the ribbon to gather the fabric, finishing with a bow. Push the bolster into the cover and thread the ribbon through the other end, again finishing with a bow.

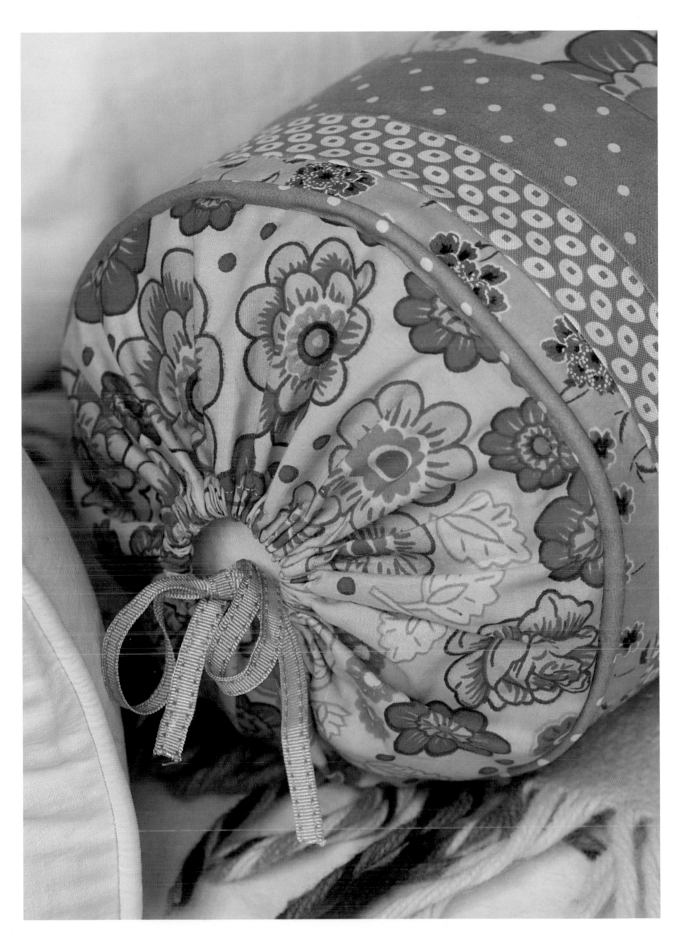

Curtain

This traditional patchwork design is made up of sets of eight triangles pieced together to form squares, which are then joined together to make a larger panel. To hang the patchwork up at a window, attach curtain clips at regular intervals across the top and thread onto a curtain pole. A curtain like this can be made to fit any size of window by simply adding more patchwork squares to the length and width. Using a lightweight wadding to line the curtain means that it will drape nicely, but will still help to prevent draughts and keep your home nice and cosy during colder weather.

The finished curtain is 105cm (42¼in) square. For a larger curtain, make more patchwork squares and add to the width or length as needed.

4 hours

MATERIALS

50 x 125cm (20 x 49in) pieces of each of eight different fabrics

110cm (43¼in) square of fabric for backing

110cm (43¼in) square of light-weight wadding

12 buttons

Needle and thread

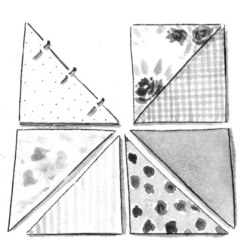

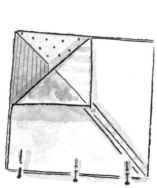

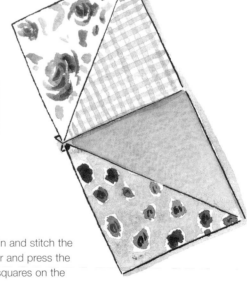

1. Using the template on page 169, cut a paper triangle for your pattern. Use this to cut nine triangles of each of the eight fabrics. Take one triangle of each fabric and lay on the work surface to form a square. With right sides together, pin and stitch the two triangles at the top left together and press the seam open. Trim the seam allowance at the corners. Repeat this with the other triangles in the square to form four small squares.

2. With right sides together, pin and stitch the two left hand squares together and press the seam open. Repeat with the squares on the right hand side.

3. Take the two strips and stitch them together with right sides together to make a square. Match up the seams neatly. Press the seam open. Repeat these steps with the remaining fabric triangles to make eight more squares, keeping the position of each fabric in each square the same.

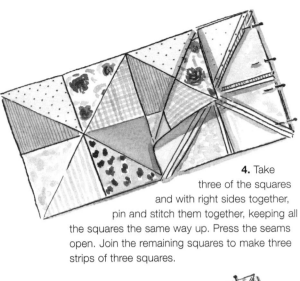

4. Take three of the squares and with right sides together, pin and stitch them together, keeping all the squares the same way up. Press the seams open. Join the remaining squares to make three strips of three squares.

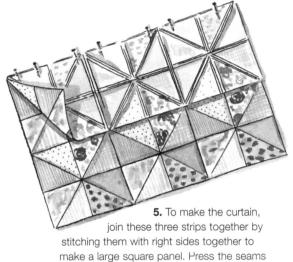

5. To make the curtain, join these three strips together by stitching them with right sides together to make a large square panel. Press the seams open. Press the front of the panel.

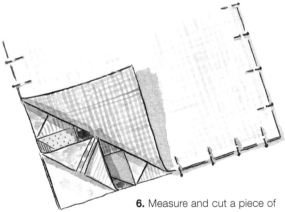

6. Measure and cut a piece of wadding and a piece of backing fabric 107cm (42⅛in) square. Lay the patchwork panel right side up onto the wadding and position the backing fabric on top of this. Ensure that all the layers are completely flat and pin and stitch all the way round leaving an opening of about 30cm (12in) along one side. Snip the corners off and turn the right way out and hand stitch the opening closed. Press. Sew buttons onto the curtain to join all the layers together at the join of the triangles.

Pouffe

There is something very satisfying about creating a piece of furniture from scraps of fabric! This pouffe is made from a nine-patch panel on the top with panels of six squares along each side; a solid square of fabric is then stitched onto the bottom (although you could make another nine-patch panel following the steps for the top). When filled with stuffing the pouffe forms a solid shape. Try recycling old blankets or woollen clothes for a more vintage look, or use squares of corduroy in different colours to striking effect.

MATERIALS
60cm (24in) squares of each of four wool fabrics
50cm (20in) square of fabric for the base
Paper for pattern
100 x 135cm (39 x 53in) of stiff iron-on interfacing
Stuffing

2 hours

1. Draw a 17cm (6¾in) square onto paper and cut out to use as your pattern to cut 33 squares of fabric (eight each of three fabrics and nine of one). Take nine of the squares and arrange them in three rows of three, making sure that no two squares of the same fabric are next to each other. With right sides together, pin and stitch three of the squares together to form a strip.

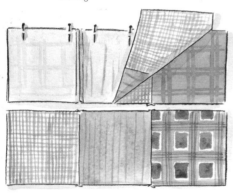

2. Repeat this with the remaining six squares to form three strips of three squares. Press the seams open. With right sides together, pin and stitch these strips together to form a square. Press the seams open. Following the manufacturer's instructions, iron stiff interfacing to the back of this panel.

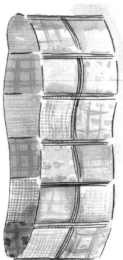

3. Join more squares together in this way to make four panels of six squares. Following the manufacturer's instructions, iron stiff interfacing to the wrong side of each panel. With right sides together, join these panels together to form a long strip two squares wide and 12 squares long. Join the ends together to form a loop.

4. With right sides together, pin and stitch this loop onto the patchwork square, lining up the seams and matching the vertical joins on the sides to the corners of the square.

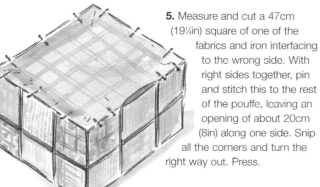

5. Measure and cut a 47cm (19¼in) square of one of the fabrics and iron interfacing to the wrong side. With right sides together, pin and stitch this to the rest of the pouffe, leaving an opening of about 20cm (8in) along one side. Snip all the corners and turn the right way out. Press.

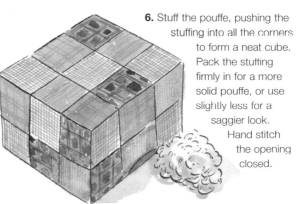

6. Stuff the pouffe, pushing the stuffing into all the corners to form a neat cube. Pack the stuffing firmly in for a more solid pouffe, or use slightly less for a saggier look. Hand stitch the opening closed.

Rug

Strip patchwork has been used to make this striking rug that mixes bold bright patterns with a small-scale gingham to create some definition. Strips of fabric in different widths create a random-looking patchwork, which has been lined with a medium weight wadding and backed with a heavy-weight cotton to help it withstand wear and tear.

2 hours

MATERIALS

Selection of different fabrics each at least 100cm (40in) long

Plain white cotton fabric at least 100cm (40in) long by the width of the finished rug

Heavy-weight cotton wadding at least 100cm (40in) long by the width of the finished rug

Fabric for the backing at least 120cm (48in) long and 20cm (8in) wider than the finished rug

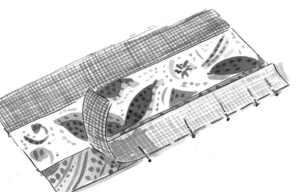

1. Measure and cut strips of fabric in varying widths all 100cm (40in) long and at least 10cm (4in) wide. Lay them onto the work surface in a pleasing arrangement. With right sides together, pin and stitch the strips together, pressing the seams open as you work. The finished panel should be about 50cm (20in) wide. Add more strips if you would like a wider rug.

2. Cut a piece of wadding and a piece of white cotton fabric to the same size as the patchwork panel. Lay the cotton onto the work surface with the wadding on the top and the patchwork on top of that. Pin all the layers together to hold them in place. Machine stitch along the seams to quilt the layers together.

3. For the backing, cut a piece of fabric measuring 120cm (48in) long and 10cm (4in) wider on each side than the patchwork panel. Press under 1cm (½in) all the way round it. Lay it on the work surface wrong side up and place the quilted patchwork panel centrally onto it, right side up. Turn over the backing fabric overlapping the raw edge of the patchwork by 1cm (½in) and pin in place to create the border. Machine stitch in place and repeat along the opposite side.

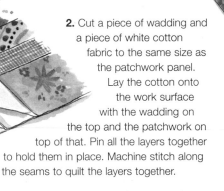

4. Repeat step 3 along the two remaining ends of the rug, pinning the border in place and machine stitching to finish. Press.

Draught Excluder

Keep the draughts at bay with this sweet draught excluder. Strips of fabric are joined together to form a long sausage shape, which is then filled with stuffing to help keep your home cosy and warm. Try to buy cotton stuffing rather than synthetic, as it is much weightier. If this is unavailable, put some dried beans or rice inside with the stuffing to make it heavier.

MATERIALS
Scraps of fabric at least 38cm (15in) long
114cm (45in) length of bobble fringe
114cm (45in) of ribbon
Stuffing

1½ hours

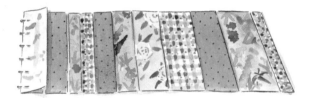

1. Cut strips of fabric in varying widths each 38cm (15in) long. Move them around until you are happy with the arrangement. With right sides together and starting at one end, pin and stitch two of the strips together. Press the seam open.

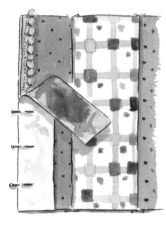

2. Continue to join the strips in this way, pressing the seams open as you go. To add the bobble fringe, lay a length of it along one raw edge of fabric (right side) and tack in position. Lay the next strip into this with right sides together and machine stitch. The finished panel should be about 85cm (34in) long (although you may wish to make a longer version for a wider door). Add more strips if you are making a longer one.

3. Pin and stitch lengths of ribbon randomly along the seams, trimming the ends to neaten them. Fold the fabric over with right sides together, pin and stitch along all three sides (not the folded side) leaving an opening of about 15cm (6in). Trim the corners and turn the right way out. Press.

4. Fill the cover with stuffing, pushing it into the corners and spreading it evenly inside. Hand stitch the opening closed.

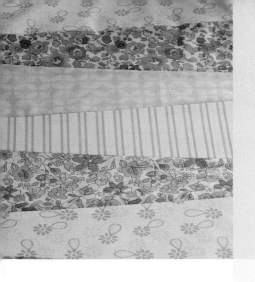

CHAPTER 2

Kitchens & Dining Rooms

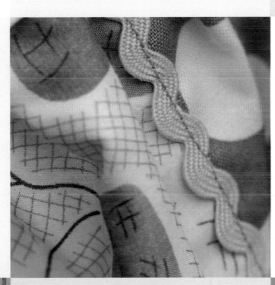

Triangle Patchwork Tablecloth

This tablecloth constructed from triangles of alternate red and off-white fabrics adds a crisp, fresh touch to a dining table. Patches of a selection of red fabrics are placed next to patches of plain fabric to unify the pattern and highlight the patchwork design. I have backed the cloth in linen, which adds a lovely weight and helps the cloth to drape beautifully. As with many of the projects in this book, the use can easily be changed – this would also make a beautiful quilt or throw.

MATERIALS

Selection of bold stripes, ginghams and patterned fabric in one basic colour
130 x 90cm (51 x 36in) piece of polka dot fabric with a pale background
120 x 160cm (47 x 63in) piece striped fabric for the backing
Paper for pattern
14 buttons

6 hours

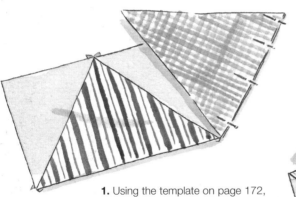

1. Using the template on page 172, cut a paper pattern triangle. Use this to cut out 56 triangles using a selection of your basic colour fabrics and a further 48 triangles in the polka dot fabric. Cut the triangle pattern in half and cut 16 half triangles from the polka dot fabric. With right sides together, pin and stitch a coloured triangle onto a polka dot half triangle, pressing the seam to the polka dot triangle side. Continue using alternate triangles until you have a strip six polka dot triangles long with a half triangle at each end.

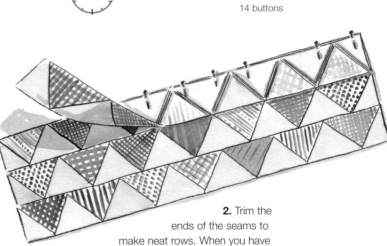

2. Trim the ends of the seams to make neat rows. When you have eight rows, with right sides together, pin and stitch them together. Press the seams open at the back. Press the whole cloth.

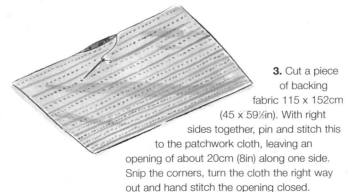

3. Cut a piece of backing fabric 115 x 152cm (45 x 59½in). With right sides together, pin and stitch this to the patchwork cloth, leaving an opening of about 20cm (8in) along one side. Snip the corners, turn the cloth the right way out and hand stitch the opening closed.

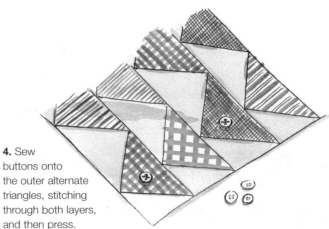

4. Sew buttons onto the outer alternate triangles, stitching through both layers, and then press.

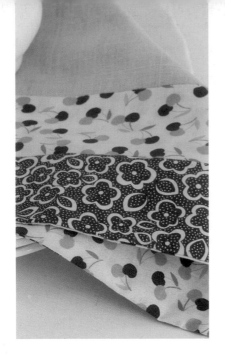

Napkin

Beautiful fabric napkins can add the finishing touch to your dining and this napkin design is so easy to make that a whole set can be created in no time at all. They are a simplified version of the traditional log cabin design, made by adding strips of fabric around a central square. A bold patterned fabric forms the border, complemented by a strong plain colour in the middle, with a more delicate pattern sandwiched between them that is used as the backing as well.

1 hour

MATERIALS

25cm (10in) piece of 115cm (45in) wide plain fabric

157cm (63in) piece of 115cm (45in) wide patterned fabric A

75cm (30in) piece of 115cm (45in) wide patterned fabric B

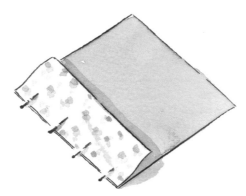

1. Measure and cut out a piece of plain fabric 19cm (7½in) square. Cut a strip of patterned fabric A measuring 6cm (2½in) wide by the width of the fabric. Cut a length of this 19cm (7½in) long and with right sides together pin and stitch it to one side of the plain fabric square with a 5mm (¼in) seam. Press the seam open.

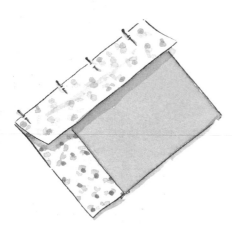

2. Cut another length from the strip of patterned fabric 24cm (9½in) long and with right sides together, pin and stitch it to the next side of the panel. Press the seam open. Cut another strip of patterned fabric 24cm (9½in) long and stitch along the third side of the panel and press the seam open. Finish with a fourth strip measuring 29cm (11½in) sewn onto the last side of the panel. Press the seam open.

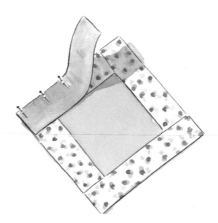

3. Cut strips of patterned fabric B again 6cm (2½in) wide from the width of the fabric. Cut a length 29cm (11½in) long and pin and stitch to one side of the patchwork panel with right sides together. Press the seam open. Cut another length of fabric 34cm (13½in) long and stitch onto the next side, with a third piece 34cm (13½in) long and a fourth piece 39cm (15½in) long to complete the patchwork.

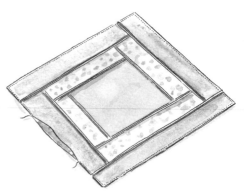

4. Cut a piece of patterned fabric A measuring 39cm (15½in) square and with right sides together pin and stitch the patchwork panel to this leaving an opening of about 5cm (2in) along one side. Snip the corners and turn the right way out. Hand stitch the opening closed and press. Repeat steps 1 to 4 to make another five napkins.

Napkin Rings

These lovely napkin rings are the perfect project for using up scraps of fabric that would otherwise be discarded. Thin strips of fabric are joined together to make a panel, which is then cut into pieces, creating a whole set that would make a unique and much treasured wedding or anniversary gift. To use up even smaller scraps of fabric, make each band separately using shorter lengths for a more individual and casual effect.

1½ hours

MATERIALS

Scraps of co-ordinating fabric

248cm (100in) rickrack braid

29 x 18cm (12 x 8in) piece of cotton wadding

4 buttons

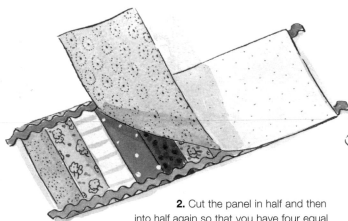

1. To make four napkin rings measure and cut 12 strips of fabric 3.5 x 26cm (1½ x 10in). Lay them on the work surface side by side and move them around until you are happy with the arrangement. With right sides together, pin and stitch the strips together with a 5mm (¼in) seam, pressing the seams open as you work.

2. Cut the panel in half and then into half again so that you have four equal size striped strips. Cut four pieces of fabric 31 x 6.5cm (12½ x 2½in). Lay a patchwork piece right side up on the work surface and lay a length of rickrack along each edge with the edge of the rickrack lined up with the raw edge of the panel. Tack in position. Lay a strip of fabric on top of this with right sides together. Machine stitch along both sides from the edge. Turn the right way out. Repeat on the other three sets of strips.

3. Turn one raw end in by 1cm (½in) and hand stitch closed. Cut a piece of wadding 29 x 4.5cm (12 x 2in) and push inside the tube of fabric making sure that it lies flat and is pushed right into the corners. Turn the remaining raw end in by 1cm (½in) and hand stitch closed.

4. Overlap the ends of the strip by 2.5cm (1in) to form a ring and hand stitch in place, finishing with a button sewn on. Repeat steps 3 and 4 for the other three napkin rings.

Placemat

2 hours

This cute flower placemat brings an element of fun to a table setting. Fabric cut into petal shapes is pieced together and finished with a central circle edged in rickrack. The mat has been lined with interfacing to make it slightly thicker, so protecting the tabletop from hot dishes and creating a more starched finish to the mat.

MATERIALS

Scraps of fabric each at least 36 x 14cm (14½ x 5½in)

35cm (14in) square of fabric for backing

Paper for pattern

35cm (14in) square of iron-on interfacing

45cm (18in) length of rickrack

1. Using the template on page 170, cut a pattern piece. Use this to cut 12 petal shapes from four different fabrics. Arrange them so that no two petals of the same colour are next to each other. With right sides together, pin and stitch three petals together and press the seams open. Repeat with the other petals.

2. With right sides together, pin and stitch two of the three-petal patches together to form a semi-circle of petals. Press the seams open. Repeat to make a second semi-circle.

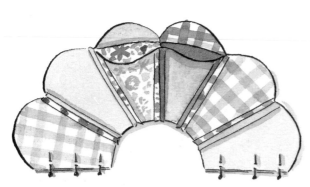

3. Lay one of the petal semi-circles onto the other one with right sides together. Pin and stitch them together and press the seams open. Press the whole patchwork on the right side.

4. Lay the patchwork flower onto the backing fabric, pin and use as a pattern to cut out the flower shape. Cut a piece of interfacing to fit this backing piece and, following the manufacturer's instructions, iron it onto the wrong side of the backing fabric. Lay the patchwork onto the backing fabric with right sides together, and pin and stitch all the way round but leaving a gap of about 3cm (1¼in). Make small snips in the seam allowance all round the flower. Turn the right way out through the gap and press.

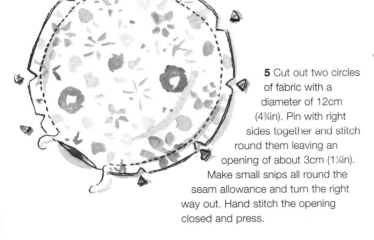

5 Cut out two circles of fabric with a diameter of 12cm (4¾in). Pin with right sides together and stitch round them leaving an opening of about 3cm (1¼in). Make small snips all round the seam allowance and turn the right way out. Hand stitch the opening closed and press.

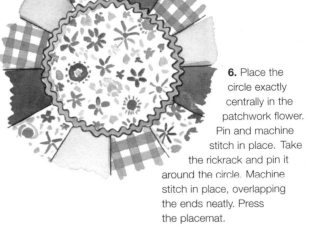

6. Place the circle exactly centrally in the patchwork flower. Pin and machine stitch in place. Take the rickrack and pin it around the circle. Machine stitch in place, overlapping the ends neatly. Press the placemat.

Table Runner

A table runner can protect your dining table as well as adding a decorative touch. This quilted version is the perfect place to put hot dishes and bowls when serving up a meal. It is made from irregular rectangles pieced together by topping and tailing them to create a long strip. Make yours long enough to fit from one end of the table to the other, with enough to hang down slightly at either end. Hand quilting can be a rather slow process but is perfect for a project of this size and holds the layers together beautifully.

3 hours

MATERIALS

60 x 40cm (24 x 16in) approx of fabric in five different designs
40 x 150cm (16 x 59in) cotton wadding
40 x 150cm (16 x 59in) piece of fabric for the backing
Embroidery thread and needle
Paper for pattern

1. Using the template on page 172, cut out a paper pattern. Pin this to the fabrics that you are using and cut out four pieces in each fabric (20 pieces in total). Arrange the pieces, topping and tailing them and ensuring that no two pieces of the same fabric are next to each other. With right sides together, pin and stitch the pieces together, pressing the seams open as you go. Continue until all 20 pieces are joined together.

2. Lay the patchwork strip onto the wadding, smoothing it out to remove any folds and creases, and cut out the shape. Repeat this using the backing fabric, making sure that the patchwork and the backing fabric are wrong sides together when you cut them out. Lay the patchwork right side up onto the wadding and then place the backing fabric right side down (if applicable) onto this. Pin and stitch all the way round, leaving an opening of about 20cm (8in) along one side.

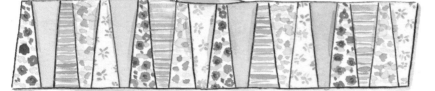

3. Snip the corners of the seams and turn the right way out. Hand stitch the opening closed and press.

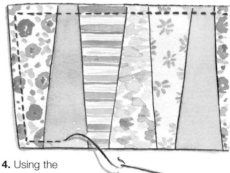

4. Using the embroidery thread, quilt through all the layers of the runner, making even stitches all the way round.

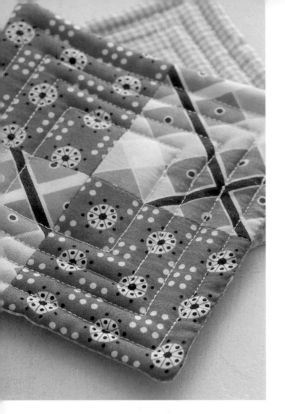

Coasters

Protect your tabletop with these cute coasters, which are the perfect project to get you into quilting. Squares of fabric are joined to make one large square, which is then backed and machine quilted. What could be easier? Use a lighter weight wadding so that the coasters lie flat.

1 hour

MATERIALS

45 x 30cm (18 x 12in) piece of fabric in each of two different designs

28 x 28cm (10 x 10in) piece of fabric in a co-ordinating design

28 x 28cm (10 x 10in) piece of wadding

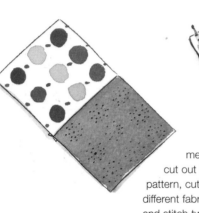

1. Draw a square on paper measuring 8cm (3in) on each side and cut out to use as a pattern. Using the pattern, cut out two squares each of two different fabrics. With right sides together, pin and stitch two of the squares (one of each fabric) together with a 1cm (½in) seam. Press the seams open.

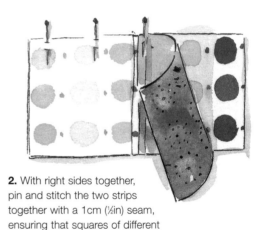

2. With right sides together, pin and stitch the two strips together with a 1cm (½in) seam, ensuring that squares of different fabrics are next to each other in a chequerboard design. Again, press the seam open.

3. Cut a square of the third fabric measuring 14cm (5in) square and cut a piece of wadding to this size. Lay the backing square right side up on the work surface with the patchwork square right side down on top of it. Place the wadding square on top of this. Pin and stitch through all layers all the way round leaving an opening of about 4cm (1½in) along one side.

4. Snip the corners and turn the right way out. Hand stitch the opening closed and press. Measure 1cm (½in) in from the edge of the coaster and mark with pins. Top stitch along this line. Measure and mark at equal intervals from this line and top stitch in the same way to quilt the coaster. Repeat steps 1 to 4 to make five more coasters.

Tea Cosy

Tea cosies need to be well insulated to keep the tea piping hot, and this pretty patchwork cosy fits the bill perfectly. The design creates a great way of using up even the smallest scraps of fabric, and works well using small-scale patterns. Create a dynamic, contemporary look by using small squares of bold prints, or solid colours in different shades. Raid your button box for a selection of pretty buttons to quilt all the layers together and add extra decoration.

MATERIALS

Scraps of fabric to cut 30 7.5cm (2¾in) squares

37 x 28cm (15 x 11in) piece of fabric for the backing

37 x 56cm (15 x 22in) piece of fabric for the lining

70cm (27in) length of bobble fringe

37 x 56cm (15 x 22in) piece of cotton wadding

Paper for pattern

12 buttons (approx.)

3 hours

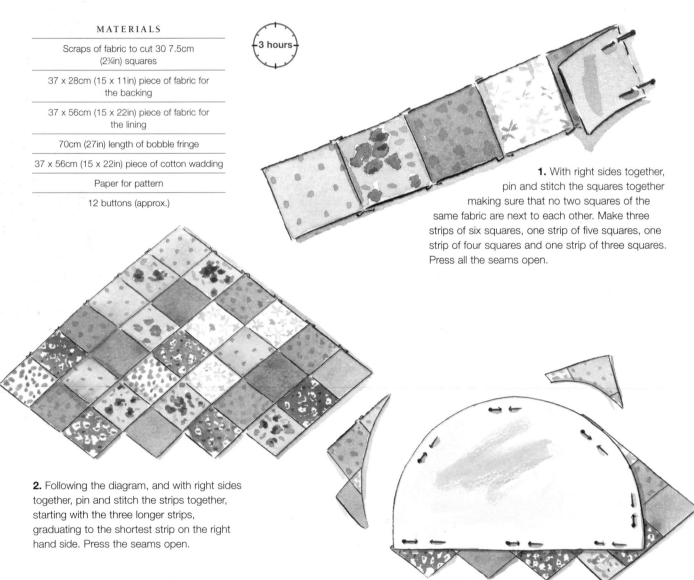

1. With right sides together, pin and stitch the squares together making sure that no two squares of the same fabric are next to each other. Make three strips of six squares, one strip of five squares, one strip of four squares and one strip of three squares. Press all the seams open.

2. Following the diagram, and with right sides together, pin and stitch the strips together, starting with the three longer strips, graduating to the shortest strip on the right hand side. Press the seams open.

3. Using the template on page 173, cut a pattern piece and lay it onto the patchwork panel centrally. Pin in place and cut out.

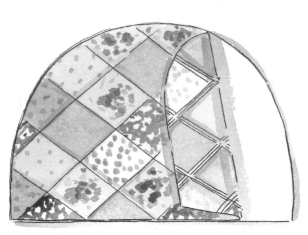

4. Using the paper pattern cut two pieces of wadding and a piece of backing fabric.

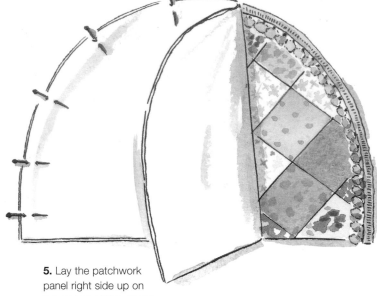

5. Lay the patchwork panel right side up on top of one of the pieces of wadding. Lay the bobble fringe all the way round the edge pointing inwards and tack in place. Lay the backing fabric right side down onto this with the other piece of wadding on top. Pin and machine stitch all the way round the curve, using the zipper foot on the machine.

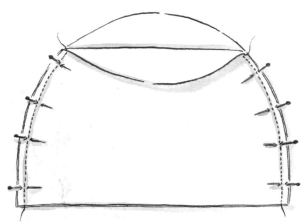

6. Using the paper pattern, cut two lining fabric pieces. With right sides together, pin and stitch them together around the curved edge only, leaving an opening of about 10cm (4in) at the top.

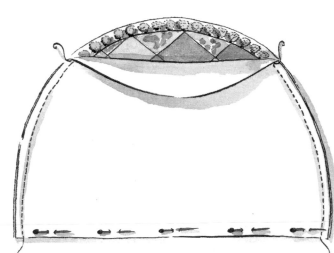

7. Slip the lining over the patchwork with right sides together lining up the seams. Pin and stitch around the base.

8. Pull the lining to its right side and hand stitch the opening closed. Push inside the tea cosy. Hand stitch buttons onto the front of the tea cosy, stitching through all the layers to hold them in place.

Apron

Sure to have you reaching for your baking tools, this cute apron is made from strip patchwork and has a real vintage feel. Strips of two different fabrics of equal width are alternated to form the 'skirt' and embellished with rickrack in a complementary colour. Add a patchwork pocket to make it practical as well as pretty, if you like.

1½ hours

MATERIALS

20cm (8in) of 137cm (54in) wide
patterned fabric

30cm (12in) of 137cm (54in) wide
spotty fabric

75cm (30in) of 137cm (54in) wide
gingham fabric

250cm (99in) rickrack braid

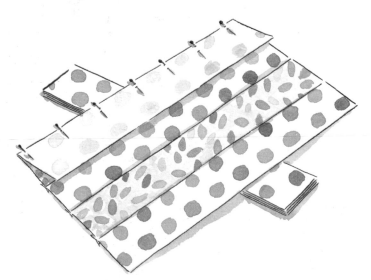

1. To make the apron, measure and cut strips of the patterned and spotty fabrics 9cm (3¾in) wide by 54cm (21½in) long. You will need five strips of spotty fabric and four strips of patterned fabric. With right sides together, pin and stitch the strips together alternating the fabrics but starting and ending with the spotty fabric. Press the seams open.

2. Cut lengths of rickrack 56cm (22in) long and pin, then stitch them along one side of each of the patterned strips. Trim the ends neatly.

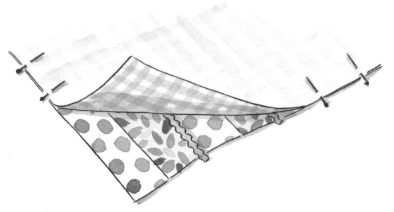

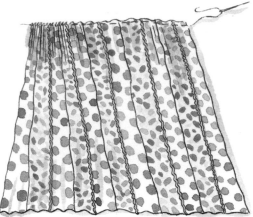

3. Cut a piece of gingham fabric 65 x 54cm (25¾ x 21½in). With right sides together, pin, then stitch this to the patchwork piece, leaving an opening about 10cm (4in) long. Snip the corners and turn the right way out through the opening. Press.

4. Make a running stitch across the top of the apron skirt and gather the fabric up to a width of about 45cm (18in). Finish with a few stitches to secure the gathering.

5. To make the waistband, measure and cut a strip of spotty fabric and a strip of gingham fabric 6.5 x 137cm (2½ x 54in). You can join lengths together if the fabric width is narrower than 137cm (54in). With right sides together, pin and stitch the strips together along both ends and one long side. Turn the right way out.

6. Press under 1cm (½in) along the raw edges of both strips of fabric. Lay the gathered edge of the apron skirt inside the centre of the waistband, placing it up from the edge by 1cm (½in), and pin in place. Top stitch along the fold to hold the apron in place, continuing round all edges of the waistband. Press.

KITCHENS AND DINING ROOMS

Kitchen Curtain

This lightweight patchwork curtain is quick to make and will transform a kitchen or utility room. Large squares of pretty floral fabrics have been teamed with crisp ticking and a plain fabric to break up the pattern. A length of curtain wire threaded through a channel across the top means it is simple to hang in place and take down to launder.

1 hour

MATERIALS

Assorted fabrics to cut into 30cm (12in) squares
Paper for pattern
Curtain wire and eyelets
2 hooks

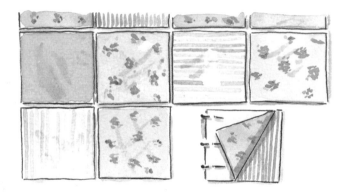

1. Measure and cut out a 30cm (12in) square of paper. Pin onto the fabrics and cut out squares. Arrange the squares so that no two squares of the same fabric are next to each other, using enough squares to create a panel of the size that you need for your curtain. With right sides together, pin and stitch the squares together working in horizontal lines.

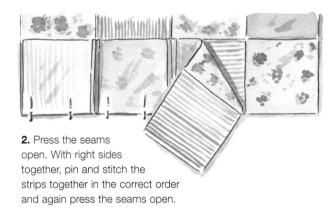

2. Press the seams open. With right sides together, pin and stitch the strips together in the correct order and again press the seams open.

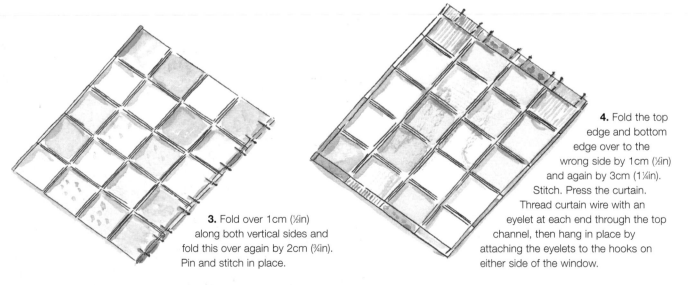

3. Fold over 1cm (½in) along both vertical sides and fold this over again by 2cm (¾in). Pin and stitch in place.

4. Fold the top edge and bottom edge over to the wrong side by 1cm (½in) and again by 3cm (1¼in). Stitch. Press the curtain. Thread curtain wire with an eyelet at each end through the top channel, then hang in place by attaching the eyelets to the hooks on either side of the window.

Trivet

Make a bright and cheerful trivet to protect your kitchen surfaces. A patchwork square is made from four triangles of fabric that, when lined with thick wadding and backed, can be quilted in a sweet flower shape for extra decoration. Choose heavier weight fabric for this project so that it will withstand heat from pans and dishes, but ensure that the fabrics are machine washable.

1 hour

MATERIALS

Piece of floral fabric

Scraps of polka dot fabric

22cm (9in) square of cotton wadding

22cm (9in) square of plain white cotton

Paper for template

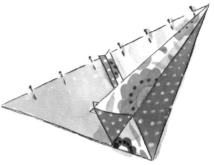

1. Using the template on page 173, cut out two triangles of floral fabric and two of polka dot fabric. With right sides together, pin and stitch a floral triangle to a polka dot triangle. Repeat with the remaining two triangles ensuring that the floral triangle is on the same side in each pair of triangles. Press the seams open.

2. With right sides together, pin and stitch the sets of triangles together. Press the seam open.

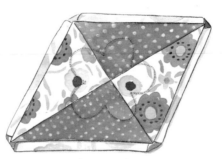

3. Cut a piece of plain white cotton and a piece of cotton wadding both measuring 22cm (9in) square. Lay the white cotton on the work surface and place the square of wadding on top of this. Put the patchwork square right side up on top of the wadding. Using the template on page 173, cut out a flower shape. Lay it centrally onto the patchwork panel and pin in place through all layers. Machine stitch around the edge of the flower.

4. Measure and cut a square of floral fabric 26cm (10½in) square. Place it right side down onto the work surface with the quilted patchwork panel centrally on top of it. Fold the corner over by 3cm (1¼in) and tuck the corner underneath the quilted panel.

5. Fold the edge of the fabric over by 1cm (½in) and press. Turn this over by another 1cm (½in) and pin in place along the quilted panel. Repeat along all the sides of the square and hand stitch in place all the way round. Press.

Dining Chair Cushion

This pretty chair cushion is made from nine blocks of fabric with alternate blocks made up of four small squares. Hand quilting has a charming quality and adds extra embellishment when done with coloured embroidery thread. A frill finishes the cushion off beautifully, with the bottom edge left unhemmed as a decorative detail.

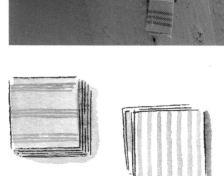

MATERIALS

30cm (12in) square of two striped fabrics for the patchwork
20 x 115cm (8 x 46in) strip of striped fabric for the frill
65 x 15cm (25½ x 6in) of striped fabric for the ties
65 x 15cm (25½ x 6in) piece of floral fabric
32cm (12½in) square of striped fabric for the backing
32cm (12½in) square of wadding
Embroidery thread and needle

3 hours

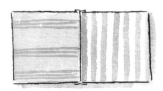

1. Measure and cut eight 7cm (2¾in) squares of both of the two striped fabrics. With right sides together, pin and stitch one square of each together, and press the seams open.

2. With right sides together, pin and stitch the two pieces from step 1 together, and press the seam open. Repeat this to make four patchwork squares.

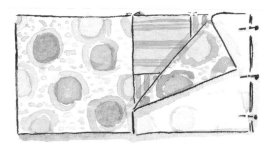

3. Using the flower fabric, measure and cut five 12cm (4¾in) squares. Take one of these and with right sides together join it to one of the patchwork squares. Stitch another flower fabric square to the other side of the patchwork square and press the seams open.

4. Make the central strip by joining two patchwork squares to either side of a flower fabric square in the same way as in step 3 and make the bottom strip as for the top. Join these three strips together to form a large square with alternating flower fabric and patchwork squares. Press the seams open.

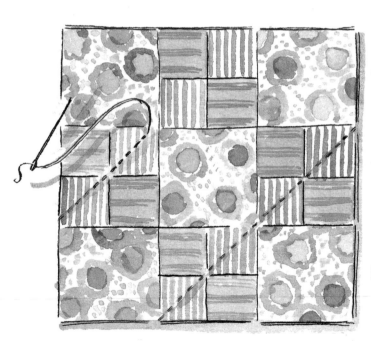

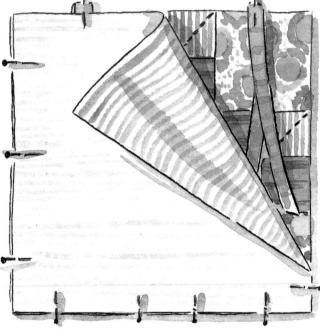

5. Cut a piece of wadding 32cm (12⅝in) square and place the patchwork on top of it. Pin the layers together. Using the embroidery thread, make a neat running stitch diagonally across the striped fabric squares.

6. Make the straps by cutting two 5 x 64cm (2 x 25in) rectangles of one of the striped fabrics, folding them in half, and folding each side into the middle. Press and stitch. Fold these in half and place on the patchwork panel as indicated. Measure and cut a piece of one of the striped fabrics for the backing. Lay this on top of the patchwork with right sides together. Pin and stitch the layers together leaving an opening of about 15cm (6in) along one side. Snip the corners and turn the right way out. Hand stitch the opening closed.

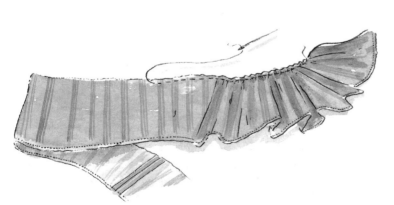

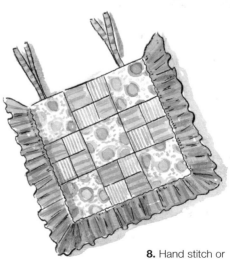

7. Tear a strip of striped fabric 9cm (3½in) wide by the width of the fabric. Join two strips together by stitching the ends together and pressing the seam open to form a strip 200cm (80in) long. Machine stitch along one side of it to prevent fraying. Make a running stitch along the other side of the strip and pull the thread to gather it so that it fits around the cushion. Sew a few stitches in the end to hold in place.

8. Hand stitch or machine stitch the frill round the cushion, turning either end under and hand stitching in place. Press carefully.

CHAPTER 3

Bedrooms

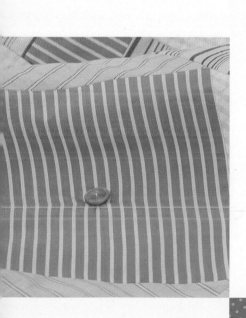

Shirting Fabric Throw

This quilt is so called because it is made from a selection of fine striped fabrics of the type often used for shirts. A central square turned on its side has been edged with triangles, which is then bordered with small squares and rectangles to create a regular pattern. The same fabric arrangements are repeated throughout the quilt.

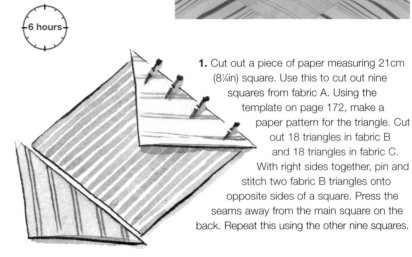

MATERIALS

80cm (31½in) square of fabric A
130 x 20cm (51 x 8in) piece of fabric B
130 x 20cm (51 x 8in) piece of fabric C
130 x 50cm (51 x 20in) piece of fabric D
115cm (45½in) square of backing fabric
Paper for pattern
115cm (45½in) square cotton wadding
9 buttons

6 hours

1. Cut out a piece of paper measuring 21cm (8¼in) square. Use this to cut out nine squares from fabric A. Using the template on page 172, make a paper pattern for the triangle. Cut out 18 triangles in fabric B and 18 triangles in fabric C. With right sides together, pin and stitch two fabric B triangles onto opposite sides of a square. Press the seams away from the main square on the back. Repeat this using the other nine squares.

2. With right sides together, pin and stitch two triangles in fabric C onto the remaining sides of the squares. Again press the seams away from the square.

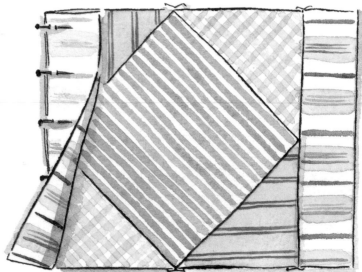

3. Cut a paper pattern rectangle 30 x 8cm (12 x 3⅛in). Use this to cut 18 strips of fabric D. Take two of these strips and with right sides together, pin and stitch them onto opposite sides of one of the patchwork squares. Press the seams open.

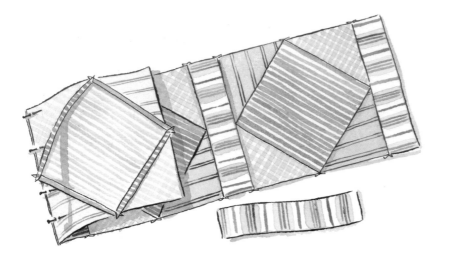

4. Pin and stitch a patchwork square onto this, with right sides together. Pin and stitch another strip to the other side of the square and continue until three patchwork squares are joined together with a strip of fabric D between each and one at each end. Keep all the squares the same way up (with fabric B at the left hand corner of each). Repeat this using the remaining six squares, to form three strips altogether.

5. Cut a paper pattern 8cm (3⅛in) square. Use this to cut 16 squares of fabric A. Take one of these squares and pin and stitch it to the end of one of the D strips, with right sides together. Pin and stitch another square onto the other end. Repeat this to form a strip of three strips of fabric D with four squares of fabric A (one at each end). Press all the seams open.

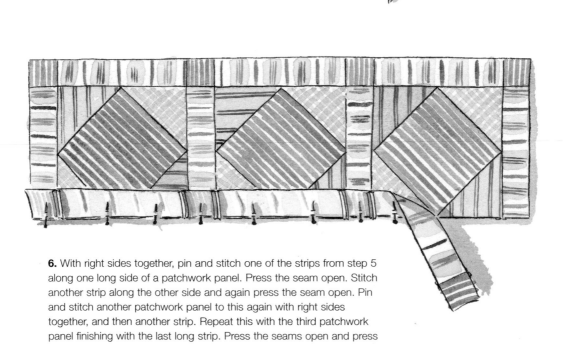

6. With right sides together, pin and stitch one of the strips from step 5 along one long side of a patchwork panel. Press the seam open. Stitch another strip along the other side and again press the seam open. Pin and stitch another patchwork panel to this again with right sides together, and then another strip. Repeat this with the third patchwork panel finishing with the last long strip. Press the seams open and press the right side of the patchwork.

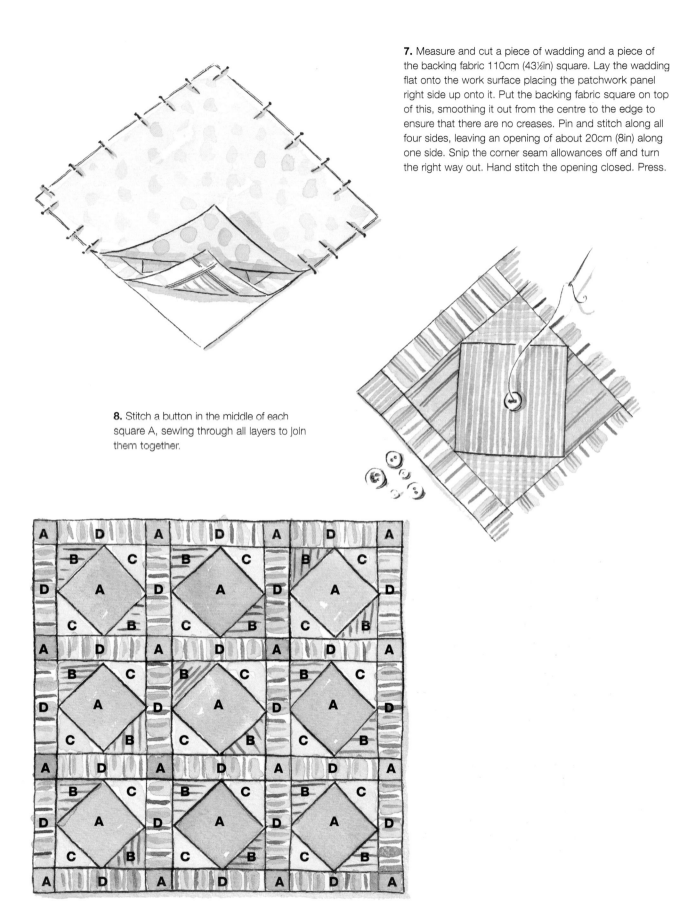

7. Measure and cut a piece of wadding and a piece of the backing fabric 110cm (43½in) square. Lay the wadding flat onto the work surface placing the patchwork panel right side up onto it. Put the backing fabric square on top of this, smoothing it out from the centre to the edge to ensure that there are no creases. Pin and stitch along all four sides, leaving an opening of about 20cm (8in) along one side. Snip the corner seam allowances off and turn the right way out. Hand stitch the opening closed. Press.

8. Stitch a button in the middle of each square A, sewing through all layers to join them together.

1½ hours

MATERIALS

6 pieces of patterned fabric each measuring 32 x 35cm (13 x 14¼in)
6 pieces of different fabrics each measuring 32 x 35cm (13 x 14¼in)
4 strips of fabric each 32 x 102cm (13 x 41in)
100 x 120cm (40 x 48in) child's duvet
Felt flowers
Embroidery thread and needle

Quilt

This project is by far the simplest quilt in this book. Using a standard store-bought duvet as its base removes the need to cut a layer of wadding and line up with backing fabric. A pretty patchwork cover is made from squares of fabric on one side, and stripes across the other, and is then filled with the duvet. It is quilted with sweet felt flowers, with knots to hold the layers together. Remove the felt flowers before machine-washing, or alternatively use buttons that can be left in place permanently.

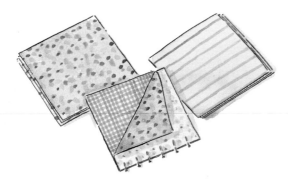

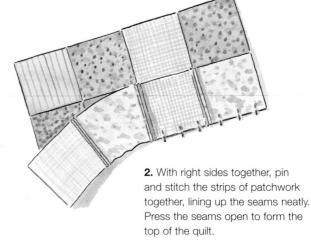

1. Cut out six pieces of patterned fabric measuring 32 x 35cm (13 x 14¼in). Cut six pieces of fabric in varying colours or patterns again measuring 32 x 35cm (13 x 14¼in). With right sides together, pin and stitch the squares together along their shorter sides, as illustrated, to make four strips of patchwork measuring 32 x 102cm (13 x 41in). Press the seams open.

2. With right sides together, pin and stitch the strips of patchwork together, lining up the seams neatly. Press the seams open to form the top of the quilt.

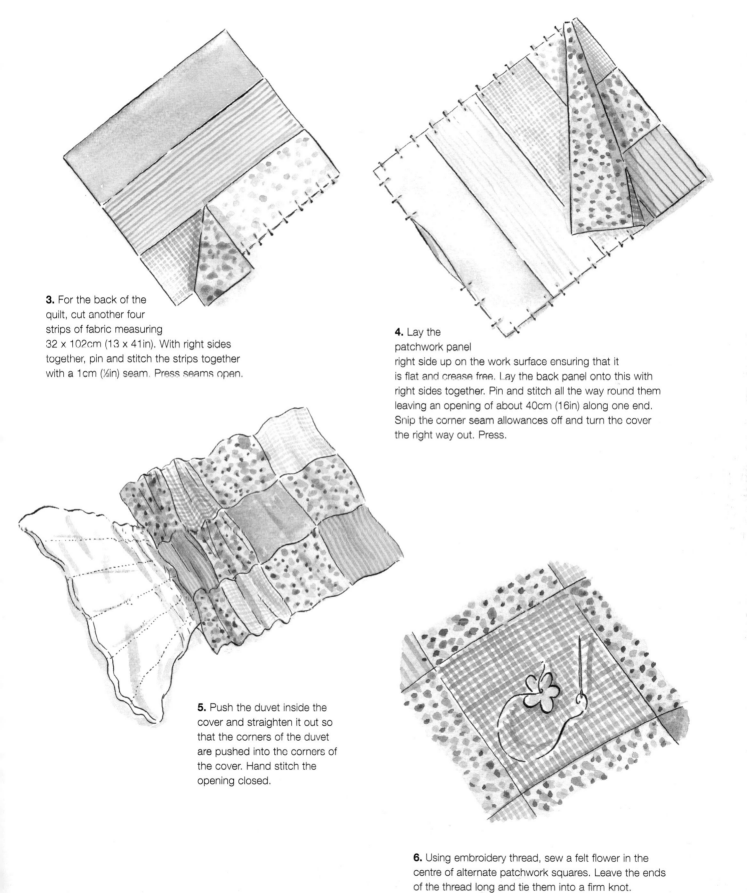

3. For the back of the quilt, cut another four strips of fabric measuring 32 x 102cm (13 x 41in). With right sides together, pin and stitch the strips together with a 1cm (½in) seam. Press seams open.

4. Lay the patchwork panel right side up on the work surface ensuring that it is flat and crease free. Lay the back panel onto this with right sides together. Pin and stitch all the way round them leaving an opening of about 40cm (16in) along one end. Snip the corner seam allowances off and turn the cover the right way out. Press.

5. Push the duvet inside the cover and straighten it out so that the corners of the duvet are pushed into the corners of the cover. Hand stitch the opening closed.

6. Using embroidery thread, sew a felt flower in the centre of alternate patchwork squares. Leave the ends of the thread long and tie them into a firm knot.

Baby Cot Quilt

Babies' bedding doesn't need to be restricted to pastel colours. Here a bold print is teamed with stripes and spots to create a contemporary-looking cot quilt made from squares of fabric joined in strips. Remember to use lightweight wadding, as young babies should not sleep under very thick covers.

3 hours

MATERIALS

50 x 90cm (20 x 36in) main colour fabric

20 x 90cm (8 x 36in) of three different co-ordinating fabrics

Piece of gingham fabric at least 82 x 70cm (32½ x 28in) for the backing

69 x 58cm (27 x 23in) cotton wadding

Embroidery thread and needle

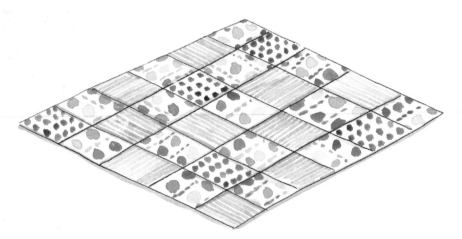

1. Cut a square paper pattern measuring 14cm (5½in). Cut out 15 squares of the main fabric, and five squares of each of the other three fabrics so that you have 30 squares in total. Arrange them on the work surface so that squares of the main fabric are laid out with three on the top line, two on the second line and so on, with squares of the other fabrics in between. There will be a block of five squares by six squares.

2. Pin a piece of paper onto the end of each line of squares, numbering them so that you will know their position. With right sides together, pin and stitch the squares together in their lines using a 1cm (½in) seam and press the seams open.

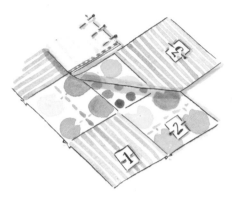

3. With right sides together, pin and stitch the strips together in the correct order using the numbers as the guide. Press the seams together.

4. Cut a piece of wadding 74 x 62cm (28 x 23½in) and lay the patchwork panel on top of it with right side up. Pin the layers together all round the edge.

5. Cut a piece of gingham fabric 82 x 70cm (32½ x 28in). Lay it onto the work surface (right side down if it has one). Place the wadding and patchwork centrally on it ensuring that there is an even border all the way round. Turn a corner over by 5cm (2in) and tuck the end under the wadding.

6. Turn under 1cm (½in) along one edge of the gingham fabric (pressing it if necessary) and then fold over and pin along the edge of the patchwork, covering the raw edge.

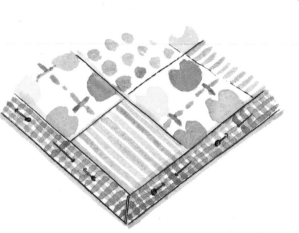

8. Hand stitch the border in place with small secure stitches. Take a length of about 40cm (16in) of embroidery thread and, using a needle, stitch from the front to the back of the quilt at a corner point leaving an end of thread about 10cm (4in) long. Stitch back up through to the front of the quilt near where the needle first went through and repeat twice more, ending with the ends of the thread at the front. Tie the ends into a secure and neat knot and trim them to about 3cm (1¼in) long. Repeat at each corner.

7. Repeat along all edges until all the border is pinned in place all around.

Duvet Cover

Duvet covers need to be made from very wide fabric that is not generally available from fabric shops in a good selection of interesting colours and patterns. Making a patchwork cover is the perfect solution; join squares of patterned and plain fabrics together to form one large panel the size that you need. Choose bold patterns mixed with a few plainer fabrics to create a contemporary patchwork design.

1½ hours

MATERIALS

Enough fabric for 18 48cm
(19in) squares

210 x 230cm (83 x 90½in) piece of fabric
for the backing

Paper for template

1. Make a paper pattern 48cm (19in) square. Use this to cut out 12 fabric squares from about five different fabrics. Fold the paper square in half to form a triangle. Use this to cut out 12 fabric triangles. Lay the squares and triangles out on a large flat surface following the illustration.

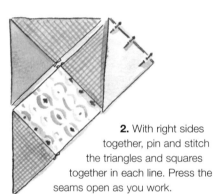

2. With right sides together, pin and stitch the triangles and squares together in each line. Press the seams open as you work.

3. Again with right sides together, pin and stitch the strips together to make one large panel, and press the seams open. Fold one side over to the wrong side by 1cm (½in) and then by another 1cm (½in). Machine stitch along the hem and press.

4. Measure and cut a piece of fabric the width of the patchwork panel by 230cm (90½in). Join two lengths together by stitching them with right sides together, pressing the seam open and then cutting it to the right width if your fabric is not wide enough. Hem one end of it as in step 3. Lay the backing fabric flat onto the work surface right side up. Place the patchwork right side down onto it, lining up three edges exactly and making sure there are no creases or folds in either layer. Fold the excess fabric from the backing over to the wrong side of the patchwork. Pin and stitch along the other three sides of both layers. Snip the corners and turn the right way out and press.

Pillowcase

Pillowcases are very easy to make. One of the nice things about making them yourself is that – with such a wide selection of fabrics available – they can be made in all sorts of lovely designs, a choice often lacking in shop-bought bed linen. Here, a bright, floral fabric is used with a jolly polka dot border and cherry trim. Having a whole set of bed linen in such a bright fabric would be a little overpowering, but a few pillowcases can liven up plain bed linen and add a more personal touch.

⏱ 1½ hours

MATERIALS
40 x 10cm (16 x 4in) pieces of two spotty fabrics
160 x 55cm (63 x 22in) piece of floral fabric
55 x 40cm (22 x 16in) piece of white fabric for the border
55cm (22in) length of braid
3 ribbons
Paper for pattern

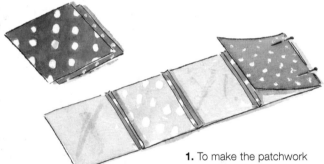

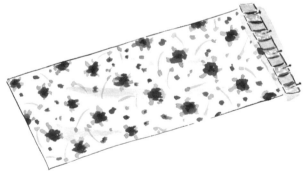

1. To make the patchwork strip, cut a paper pattern 7cm (2½in) square. Pin onto both of the spotty fabrics and cut out five squares of each fabric. With right sides together, pin and stitch the squares together to form a long strip alternating the different spotty fabrics. Press the seams open.

2. Measure and cut out a piece of floral fabric 52 x 157cm (20½ x 62in). With right sides together, pin and stitch the patchwork strip to one end of the floral strip. Press the seam towards the spotty fabric.

3. Measure and cut a piece of white fabric 52 x 36cm (20½ x 14¼in). With right sides together, pin and stitch this to the patchwork strip. Press the seam open.

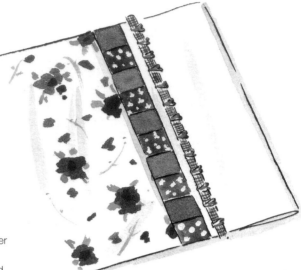

4. Fold the other side of the white fabric under 1cm (½in) to the wrong side and press. With wrong side facing upwards, line up the folded edge with the stitching line joining the floral fabric to the spotty patchwork strip. Pin and hand stitch in place.

5. With right side upwards, take the braid and pin it to the white border about 1cm (½in) from the spotty fabric strip. Machine stitch it in place sewing along both edges of the braid.

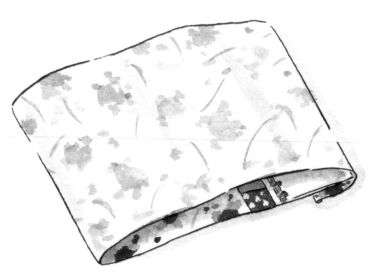

6. Fold the raw edge of the floral fabric over to the wrong side by 1cm (½in) and fold this over again by 2cm (1in). Pin and stitch a few millimetres (⅛in) from the first fold. Press.

7. Lay the fabric panel onto the work surface right side up. Measure and make a fold 75cm (29½in) from the edge of the white border fabric. Fold the fabric over the top with right sides together and fold the excess at the patchwork end underneath all the layers neatly. Pin and stitch along both sides. Turn the right way out and press.

Crazy Nine-patch Cushion

This cushion is made using a technique called crazy nine-patch and looks much more complicated than it is. Nine squares of different fabrics are cut and the layers mixed up to give you nine patchwork squares, each containing a block of all of the fabrics in different arrangements. It is great fun to make and produces a lovely effect, which could be used to produce a beautiful quilt when more blocks are made – or any number of other projects.

1 day

MATERIALS

21cm (8⅜in) squares of each of nine different fabrics
25 x 70cm (10 x 28in) piece of fabric for the border
70 x 110cm (28 x 43in) piece of fabric for the backing
Metal ruler
Rotary cutter
65cm (25½in) square cushion pad

1. Lay the nine squares on top of each other making sure that they are exactly lined up. Take the rotary cutter and ruler and make a cut through all the layers at an angle as shown.

2. Take the top layer of the side strip and place it on the bottom of the pile. With right sides together, pin and stitch a main piece to the side strip next to it. Repeat with all nine layers, keeping them in order. Press the seams open.

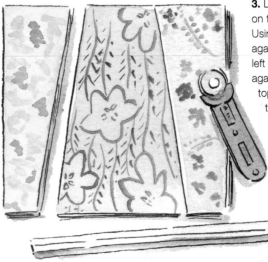

3. Lay the nine squares exactly on top of each other in order. Using the rotary cutter and ruler again, make another cut on the left hand side of the square again at an angle, wider at the top than the bottom. Take the top two layers of the side strip and put them on the bottom of the pile. With right sides together, pin and stitch each side strip to the main piece next to it, pressing the seams open and keeping them in order.

4. With all the layers neatly stacked again, turn the pile around so that the seams run horizontally. Using the rotary cutter and ruler make a third cut through all the layers at an angle so that the side strip is narrower at the top than the bottom. You may need to run the cutter along the line several times, to cut through all the fabric and seams.

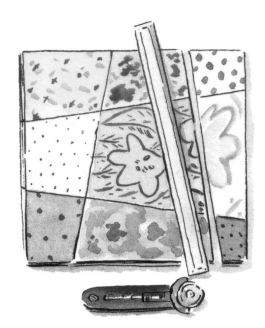

5. Take the top three layers of the side strip and put them at the bottom of the pile as before, and stitch each main piece to its side strip as before. Press the seams open.

6. Turn the pile of squares around again and cut a fourth strip with the top being wider than the bottom, as before. Take the top six layers and put them at the bottom of the pile. Sew both pieces from each layer together as before and press the seams open.

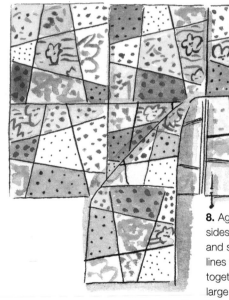

7. You will now have nine patchwork squares with a piece of each of the nine fabrics on each one. Trim each square to straighten up the sides and seams. Lay the squares in a block of three by three. With right sides together, pin and stitch the top three squares together, and repeat with the other two lines of three squares. Press the seams open.

8. Again with right sides together, pin and stitch the three lines of squares together to form one large square. Press the seams open.

9. Cut two strips of a co-ordinating fabric 5.5 x 59cm (2 x 23⅝in) long. With right sides together, pin and stitch a strip onto two opposite sides of the patchwork square. Press the seams open.

10. Measure and cut two more strips of fabric 5.5 x 66cm (2 x 26⅝in) long. Pin and stitch them onto the two remaining sides of the patchwork square, with right sides together. Press the seams open.

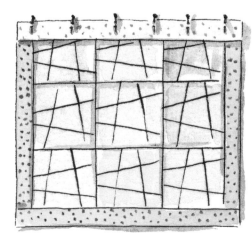

11. To make the back of the cushion, cut two rectangles of fabric measuring 66 x 50cm (26⅜ x 20in). Turn under 1cm (½in) along one long side of both pieces and turn under another 2cm (1in). Pin and stitch along the first fold and press.

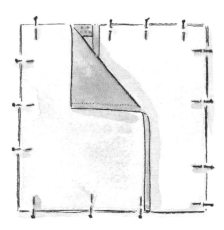

12. Lay the patchwork square right side up onto the work surface. Lay one of the back rectangles onto this right side down, matching up the raw edges. Lay the other rectangle on top of this with right side down, again matching up the raw edges. Pin and stitch all the way round the square. Snip the corner seam allowance off and turn the cushion cover the right way out. Press, and then fill with the cushion pad.

Blue Quilt

The graphic look of this quilt is achieved by using classic checks and stripes with a bold solid colour as the central block. Adding borders to a large central panel is a quick and easy way of creating a quilt and gives an eye-catching look that would work equally well on a sofa or armchair as on a bed.

1 day

MATERIALS

65cm (26in) square of blue fabric for the centre panel

80 x 45cm (31½ x 18in) piece of checked fabric

100 x 50cm (39½ x 20in) piece of striped fabric

115 x 45cm (46 x 18in) piece of spotty fabric

115cm (46in) square of fabric for backing

115cm (46in) square of wadding

Embroidery thread and needle

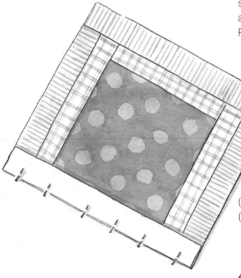

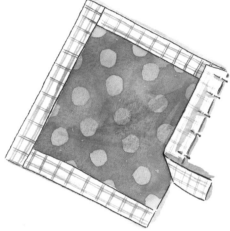

1. Measure and cut a central panel 60cm (24in) square. Cut two strips of checked fabric 10 x 60cm (4 x 24in). With right sides together, pin and stitch the strips along opposite sides of the main panel. Press the seams open.

2. Measure and cut two more strips of checked fabric 10 x 79cm (4 x 32in). With right sides together, pin and stitch them along the other two sides of the main strip. Press the seams open.

3. Cut two strips of striped fabric 10 x 79cm (4 x 32in), and two more strips 10 x 97cm (4 x 39in). Join them in the same way as before. Cut two strips of spotty fabric measuring 10 x 97cm (4 x 39in) and two more of 10 x 115cm (4 x 46in), joining these as before.

4. Measure and cut a piece of wadding and a piece of backing fabric 115cm (46in) square. Lay the patchwork right side up onto the wadding and the backing fabric with right side down onto this. Pin and stitch the three layers together all the way round leaving an opening of about 30cm (12in). Trim the corners and turn the right way out. Hand stitch the opening closed and press. Stitch knots at the corners of the strips to quilt it.

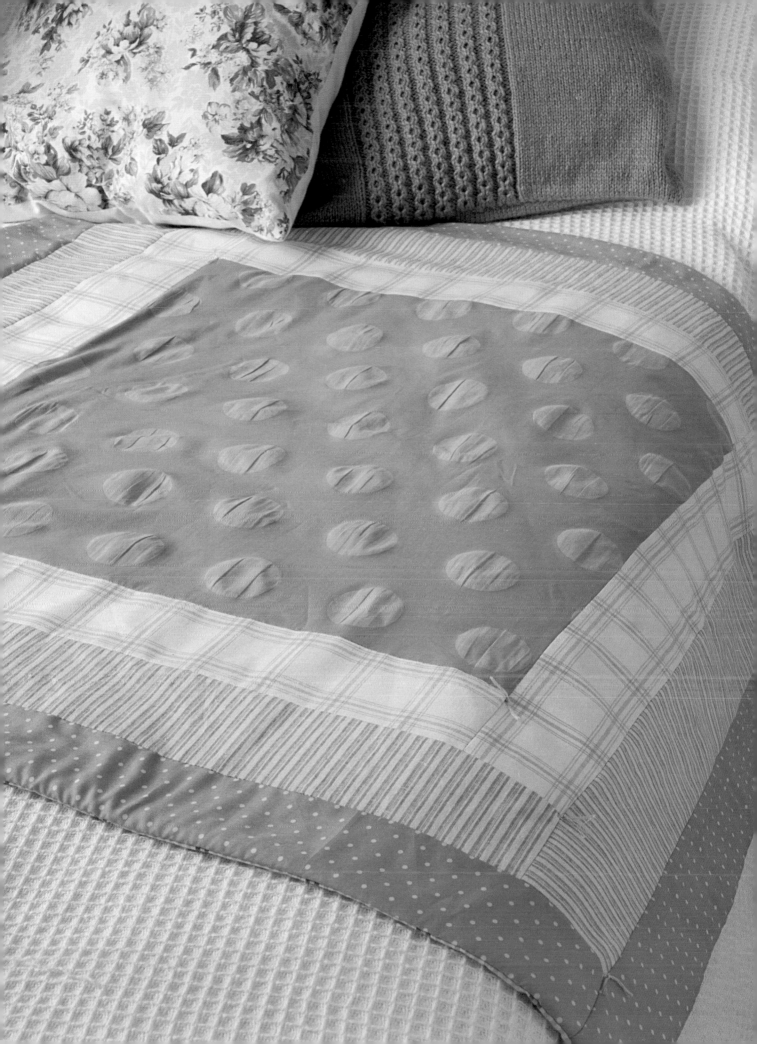

Pretty Quilt

5 hours

Patchwork has long been used as an economical way of producing beautiful home furnishings, using scraps of new and old fabrics. This charming quilt is made from squares of lots of different fabrics left over from other sewing projects, mixed with a plain linen fabric to unify the many patterns. Choosing fabrics with one or two colours in common will create a more harmonious effect, but the beauty of this design is that any fabric will work to create a lovely mismatched old-fashioned feel.

MATERIALS

15cm (6in) squares of a mixture of patterned fabrics, 54 squares in total
90 x 135cm (36 x 54in) piece of plain fabric
110 x 145cm (43 x 57in) piece of wadding
30 x 145cm (12 x 57in) piece of fabric for the binding
110 x 145cm (43 x 57in) piece of fabric for the backing
Embroidery thread and needle
Paper for the markers

1. Cut a 13cm (5in) square paper pattern. Using this, cut out 54 squares of plain fabric and 54 squares of patterned fabrics. Arrange them on the work surface, alternating plain and patterned squares until you are happy with the arrangement.

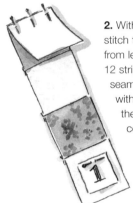

2. With right sides together, pin and stitch the squares together working from left to right vertically to form 12 strips of nine squares. Press the seams open, and label each strip with a number (pinning paper to the bottom of each) to keep the correct order.

3. With right sides together, pin and stitch the strips together working from the left to the right hand side. Press the seams open as you go. Remove the numbers and press the whole patchwork panel.

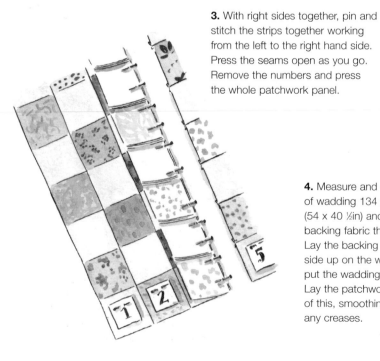

4. Measure and cut a piece of wadding 134 x 101cm (54 x 40 ½in) and a piece of backing fabric the same size. Lay the backing fabric wrong side up on the work surface and put the wadding on top of this. Lay the patchwork panel on top of this, smoothing it out to remove any creases.

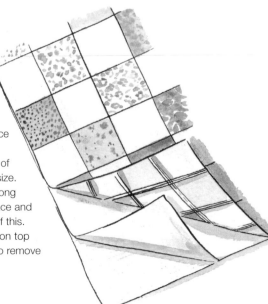

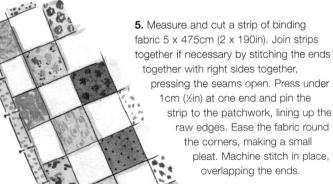

5. Measure and cut a strip of binding fabric 5 x 475cm (2 x 190in). Join strips together if necessary by stitching the ends together with right sides together, pressing the seams open. Press under 1cm (½in) at one end and pin the strip to the patchwork, lining up the raw edges. Ease the fabric round the corners, making a small pleat. Machine stitch in place, overlapping the ends.

6. Snip the corners off. Press under 1cm (½in) along the remaining raw edge of the binding strip. Pin this folded edge onto the back of the quilt and hand stitch in place.

CHAPTER 4

Work & Play Spaces

MATERIALS

35 x 45cm (14 x 18in) of each of two fabrics for the star
45cm (18in) square of fabric for the backing and ties
50 x 40cm (20 x 16in) piece (approx) of spotty fabric
40cm (16in) square (approx) of checked fabric
30cm (12in) square of washable heavy-weight wadding
120cm (47in) of bobble fringe
Paper for pattern

3 hours

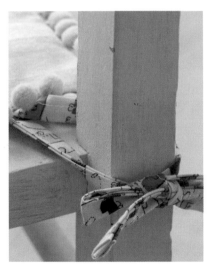

Child's Seat Cushion

Making a cushion for a simple wooden chair can add a lovely decorative touch. This patchwork star is a slightly more complex design, but can easily be made using a sewing machine. It can be made to fit any size of seat by increasing the size of the templates accordingly. A cute bobble fringe finishes the cushion off beautifully, with fabric ties added to hold it in place.

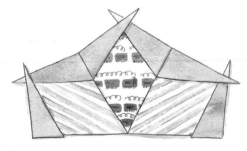

2. With right sides together, pin and stitch three of the shapes made in step 1 together, alternating the different fabrics to form two semi-circles. Press all the seams open.

1. Using the template on page 169, cut out pattern pieces A, B and C. Cut out three pieces of A from each of the two different fabrics. Cut out 12 pieces of B in one fabric. With right sides together, pin and stitch one B piece along one edge of an A piece. Press the seam open. Stitch another B piece along the next side of the A piece and again press the seam open. Continue joining two B pieces to each of the six A pieces.

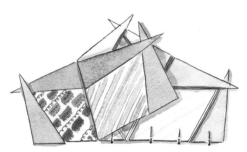

3. Again with right sides together, pin and stitch these two pieces together, and press the seam open. Trim off any bits of seam allowance that stick out round the edge.

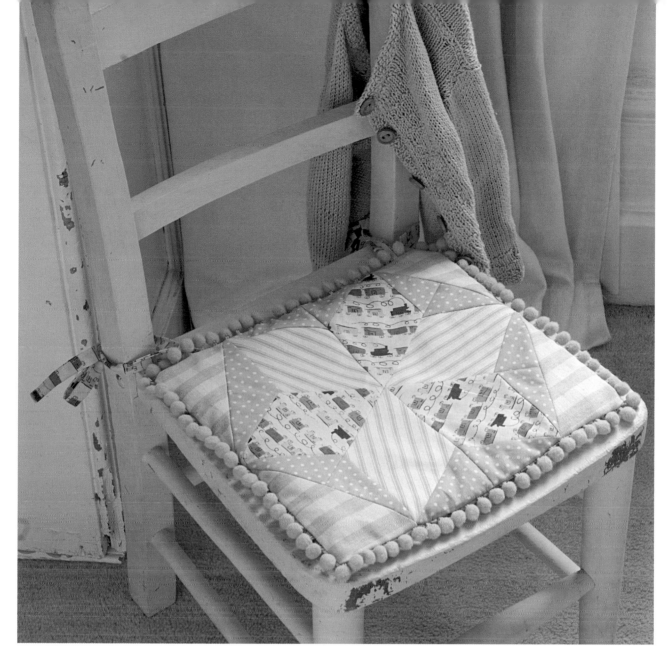

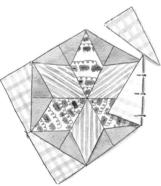

4. Lay the patchwork star onto the work surface with one of its points at the top. Using pattern piece C, cut four triangles from the checked fabric. With right sides together, pin and stitch them onto the top and bottom corners of the star. Press the seams open.

5. Measure and cut two 4 x 45cm (1½ x 18in) strips of one of the fabrics. Fold them both in half along their length and press. Fold the edges into the centre fold and press. Pin and stitch along the length of both to form the ties.

6. Cut a piece of backing fabric the same size as the patchwork panel. Pin and tack the bobble fringe all the way round the right side of the patchwork panel, with the bobbles pointing inwards. Fold the ties in half and position them at the top of the patchwork panel a few centimetres from both top corners. Place the backing fabric right sides together onto the patchwork and pin and stitch all the way round leaving an opening of about 10cm (4in) along the top edge. Turn the right way out. Cut a piece of wadding to fit the cover and push in place. Hand stitch the opening closed. Press.

Play Mat

Six different fabrics have been used to make this baby's play mat. Polka dots and checks in similar colours create a harmonious look that is as practical as it is attractive. With a patchwork-pieced star at the centre, it is built up with strips of fabric around the sides and squares at the corners. Use a synthetic wadding (or cotton wadding that is machine washable) so that the mat can be laundered regularly.

MATERIALS

60 x 20cm (23 x 8in) piece of fabric A
30 x 50cm (12 x 20in) piece of fabric B
30 x 60cm (12 x 23½in) piece of fabric C
30cm (12in) square of fabric D
45 x 60cm (18 x 23½in) piece of fabric E
60 x 90cm (23½ x 35½in) piece of fabric F
90cm (35½in) square of fabric for backing
90cm (35½in) square of heavy-weight wadding
Paper for pattern pieces

⊢1½ hours⊣

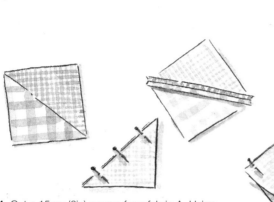

1. Cut a 15cm (6in) square from fabric A. Using the template on page 172, cut out a paper pattern triangle. Use this to cut out eight triangles from the remainder of fabric A and eight triangles from fabric B. With right sides together, pin and stitch one of each together and press the seams open to form eight squares.

2. With right sides together, pin and stitch two of the squares together with the two triangles of fabric B next to each other. Repeat this with the other squares to form four rectangles. Press the seams open. Take two of the rectangles and pin and stitch them onto opposite sides of the A fabric square from step 1. Press the seams open.

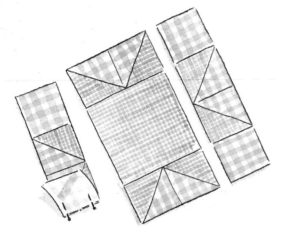

3. Using fabric B again, cut four 8cm (3¼in) squares. Pin and stitch two of them onto each end of the two remaining rectangles with right sides together. Press the seams open. Again with right sides together, pin and stitch these strips onto the two remaining raw sides of the central square, matching up the seams. Press the seams open.

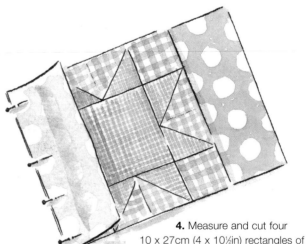

4. Measure and cut four 10 x 27cm (4 x 10½in) rectangles of fabric C and pin and stitch two of them onto opposite sides of the patchwork panel with right sides together.

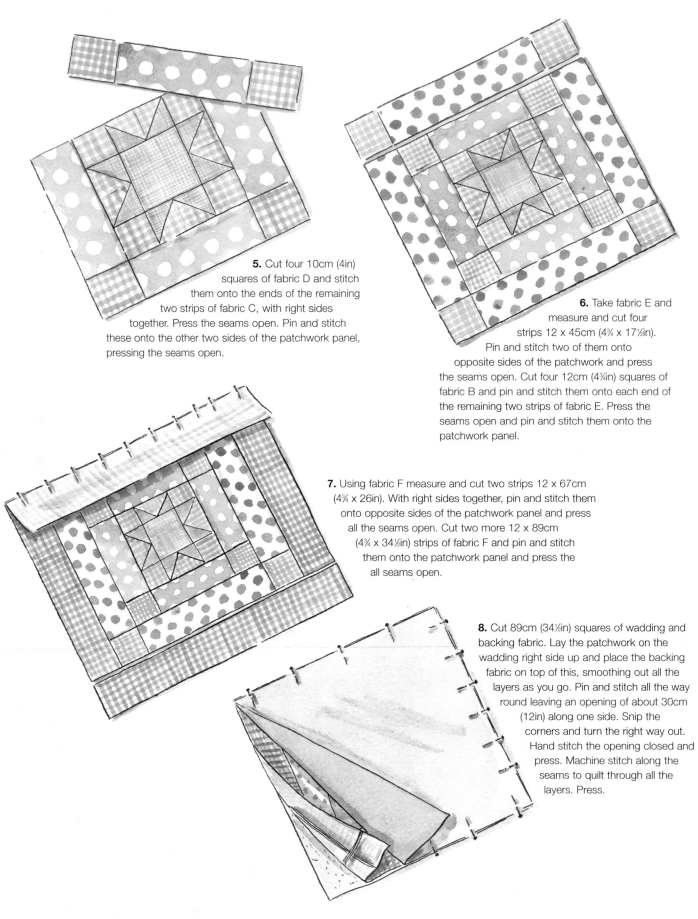

5. Cut four 10cm (4in) squares of fabric D and stitch them onto the ends of the remaining two strips of fabric C, with right sides together. Press the seams open. Pin and stitch these onto the other two sides of the patchwork panel, pressing the seams open.

6. Take fabric E and measure and cut four strips 12 x 45cm (4¾ x 17½in). Pin and stitch two of them onto opposite sides of the patchwork and press the seams open. Cut four 12cm (4¾in) squares of fabric B and pin and stitch them onto each end of the remaining two strips of fabric E. Press the seams open and pin and stitch them onto the patchwork panel.

7. Using fabric F measure and cut two strips 12 x 67cm (4¾ x 26in). With right sides together, pin and stitch them onto opposite sides of the patchwork panel and press all the seams open. Cut two more 12 x 89cm (4¾ x 34½in) strips of fabric F and pin and stitch them onto the patchwork panel and press the all seams open.

8. Cut 89cm (34½in) squares of wadding and backing fabric. Lay the patchwork on the wadding right side up and place the backing fabric on top of this, smoothing out all the layers as you go. Pin and stitch all the way round leaving an opening of about 30cm (12in) along one side. Snip the corners and turn the right way out. Hand stitch the opening closed and press. Machine stitch along the seams to quilt through all the layers. Press.

Child's Cushion

This pretty patchwork cushion is perfect for a girl's bedroom. Three fabrics are pieced together to form a square, which is then backed with wadding and quilted to make an even softer cushion. The decorative trim is made from strips of unhemmed fabric, gathered and stitched along the seams, with a fabric rosette to finish.

6 hours

MATERIALS

50 x 18cm (20 x 7in) of each of three different fabrics for the front

50cm (20in) square of plain backing fabric

50cm (20in) square of cotton wadding

90 x 115cm (36 x 45in) of fabric for the back and frills

Needle and thread

Button

50cm (20in) square cushion pad

Masking tape

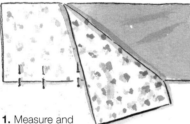

1. Measure and cut three rectangles of different fabrics 50 x 18cm (20 x 7in). With right sides together, pin and stitch them together along the long sides to form a square. Press the seams open.

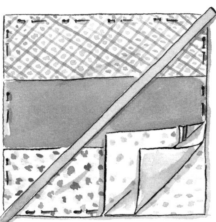

2. Cut a piece of fabric and a piece of wadding 50cm (20in) square. Lay the backing fabric right side down on the work surface with the wadding on top. Place the patchwork panel right side up onto this and smooth out all the layers. Pin the layers together. Stick masking tape from one corner to the opposite corner and stitch along one side of it.

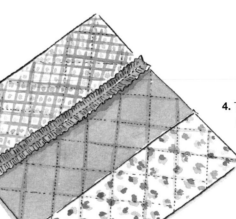

3. Continue to stick masking tape onto the fabric, spacing each strip 8cm (3¼in) from the previous stitch line and stitching along it, until you reach each corner. Then repeat this process working from the other corners so that the panel is quilted.

4. Tear a strip of fabric 4cm (1½in) wide by the width of the fabric you are using and make a running stitch centrally along its length. Gather the strip and pin along one of the seams on the patchwork. Make another gathered strip for the other seam. Machine stitch the gathered strips in place.

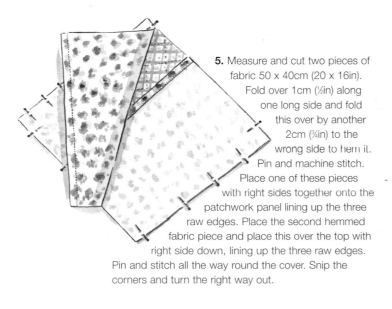

5. Measure and cut two pieces of fabric 50 x 40cm (20 x 16in). Fold over 1cm (½in) along one long side and fold this over by another 2cm (¾in) to the wrong side to hem it. Pin and machine stitch. Place one of these pieces with right sides together onto the patchwork panel lining up the three raw edges. Place the second hemmed fabric piece and place this over the top with right side down, lining up the three raw edges. Pin and stitch all the way round the cover. Snip the corners and turn the right way out.

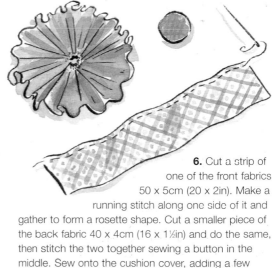

6. Cut a strip of one of the front fabrics 50 x 5cm (20 x 2in). Make a running stitch along one side of it and gather to form a rosette shape. Cut a smaller piece of the back fabric 40 x 4cm (16 x 1½in) and do the same, then stitch the two together sewing a button in the middle. Sew onto the cushion cover, adding a few strips of fabric hanging down for extra decoration. Fill the cover with the cushion pad.

Toy Bag

Drawstring bags are great for storing toys in and can be hung up out of the way at the end of the day. This bold print has been enhanced with a pretty patchwork panel edged in a chunky rickrack braid. These bags don't need to be restricted to just toys – they can be made in any size to house all sorts of things from laundry, clothes and shoes to toiletries and cosmetics, by altering the dimensions to the size required.

⊢6 hours⊣

MATERIALS

80 x 100cm (32 x 40in) piece of main fabric for bag
40 x 30cm (16 x 12in) pieces of each of two fabrics for patchwork
30 x 60cm (12 x 24in) piece of fabric for the top lining
20 x 60cm (8 x 24in) piece of gingham fabric
110cm (44in) length of rickrack
250cm (99in) length of ribbon
Safety pin

1. Measure and cut six 10cm (3½in) squares of two different fabrics. With right sides together, pin and stitch them together to make two rows of six squares, alternating the fabrics. Press the seams open.

2. With right sides together, pin and stitch the two strips together, matching up the seams. Press the seam open.

3. Measure and cut two strips of gingham 5 x 55cm (1¾ x 22in). With right sides together, pin and stitch them onto either side of the patchwork panel. Press the seams open.

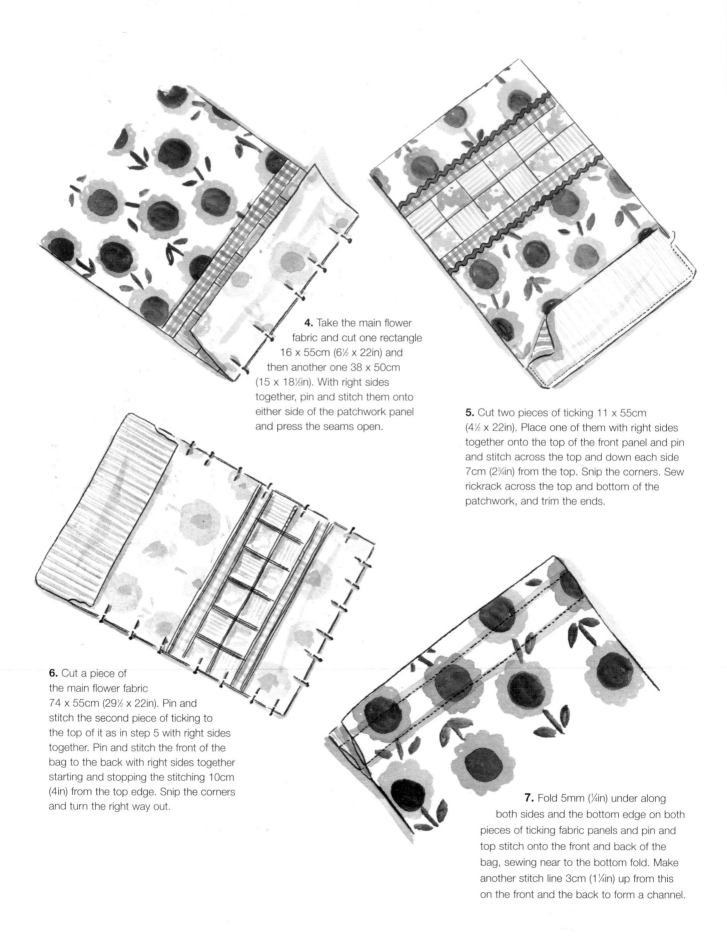

4. Take the main flower fabric and cut one rectangle 16 x 55cm (6½ x 22in) and then another one 38 x 50cm (15 x 18½in). With right sides together, pin and stitch them onto either side of the patchwork panel and press the seams open.

5. Cut two pieces of ticking 11 x 55cm (4½ x 22in). Place one of them with right sides together onto the top of the front panel and pin and stitch across the top and down each side 7cm (2¾in) from the top. Snip the corners. Sew rickrack across the top and bottom of the patchwork, and trim the ends.

6. Cut a piece of the main flower fabric 74 x 55cm (29½ x 22in). Pin and stitch the second piece of ticking to the top of it as in step 5 with right sides together. Pin and stitch the front of the bag to the back with right sides together starting and stopping the stitching 10cm (4in) from the top edge. Snip the corners and turn the right way out.

7. Fold 5mm (¼in) under along both sides and the bottom edge on both pieces of ticking fabric panels and pin and top stitch onto the front and back of the bag, sewing near to the bottom fold. Make another stitch line 3cm (1¼in) up from this on the front and the back to form a channel.

8. Thread a safety pin through the end of the ribbon and feed it through the channel on the front and back of the bag and tie the ends in a knot at one side. Thread another length of ribbon through from the other side front and back again and again tie the ends in a knot, on the other side. Pull both ribbons to gather up the bag. Sew a loop of ribbon to the back of the bag to hang it up.

Baby's Ball

This is a great present to make as a gift for a newborn and is nice and easy to do. Choose fabrics with a small print, or try large, bold bright fabrics to really catch a baby's eye. When making items for children, a good starting point for fabrics can be children's clothes that have been outgrown, as they are often in small prints that work well for projects like this. The ball is filled with synthetic stuffing so that it is machine washable. Place a bell in the middle as you stuff, to keep the baby well entertained.

2 hours

MATERIALS

Assorted scraps of fabric to cut into 12cm (5in) pentagons

Stiff paper for the backing

Needle and thread

Stuffing

Bell

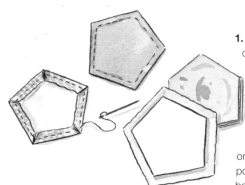

1. Using the template on page 168, cut out 12 backing papers using the stiff paper. Pin them onto the wrong side of the fabric and cut out, adding an extra 1cm (½in) all the way round to make 12 pentagons. Fold over the 1cm (½in) of the fabric onto the paper and tack in position. Repeat with all 12 paper backed pentagons.

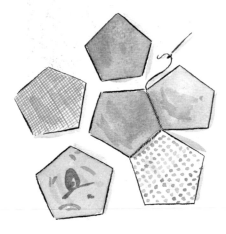

2. Lay one of the pentagons right side up on the work surface and arrange five of the others around it. With right sides together whipstitch each edge together. Repeat with the remaining six pentagons.

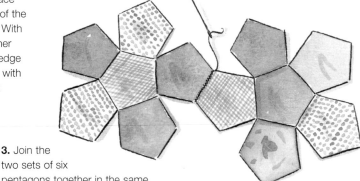

3. Join the two sets of six pentagons together in the same way, whipstitching along all the edges together to form a sphere. Leave one side open.

4. Remove the tacking stitches from each pentagon and remove the backing papers. Turn the ball the right way out. Stuff the ball, packing the stuffing in to create a good shape and adding a bell in the middle. Hand stitch the opening closed.

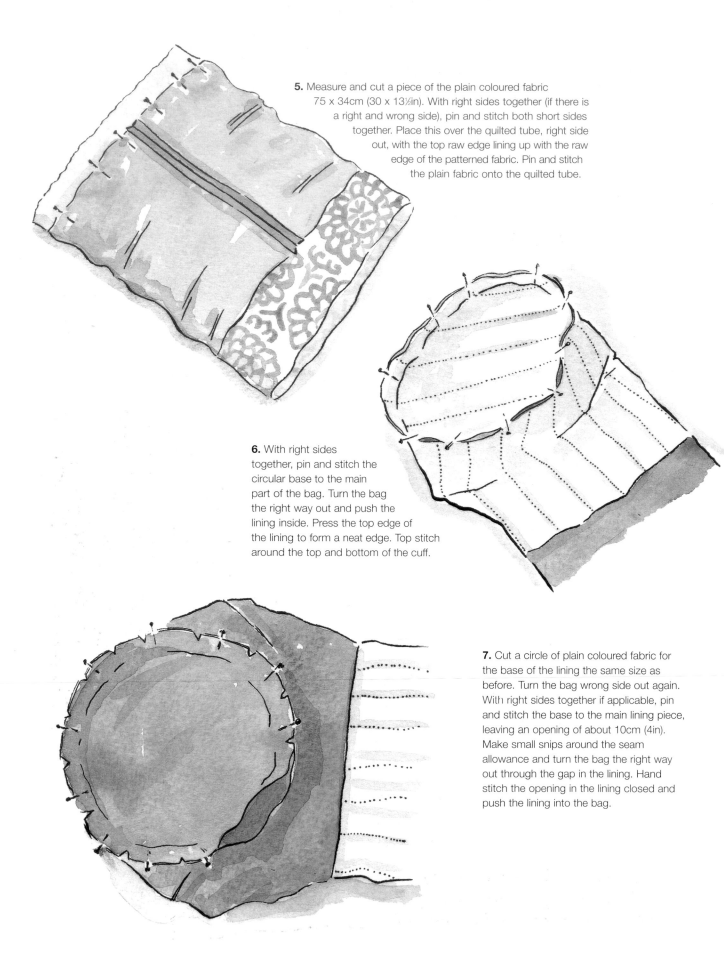

5. Measure and cut a piece of the plain coloured fabric 75 x 34cm (30 x 13½in). With right sides together (if there is a right and wrong side), pin and stitch both short sides together. Place this over the quilted tube, right side out, with the top raw edge lining up with the raw edge of the patterned fabric. Pin and stitch the plain fabric onto the quilted tube.

6. With right sides together, pin and stitch the circular base to the main part of the bag. Turn the bag the right way out and push the lining inside. Press the top edge of the lining to form a neat edge. Top stitch around the top and bottom of the cuff.

7. Cut a circle of plain coloured fabric for the base of the lining the same size as before. Turn the bag wrong side out again. With right sides together if applicable, pin and stitch the base to the main lining piece, leaving an opening of about 10cm (4in). Make small snips around the seam allowance and turn the bag the right way out through the gap in the lining. Hand stitch the opening in the lining closed and push the lining into the bag.

8. Cut a strip of patterned fabric 58 × 10cm (23 × 4in). Cut a piece of interfacing to the same size and following the manufacturer's instructions attach it to the wrong side of the fabric strip. Fold the strip in half along its length and stitch along one short end and along the length. Snip the corners. Turn the tube the right way out and press. Turn the raw end in and top stitch all the way round the handle. Sew the handle onto the bag finishing with a button at each end of it.

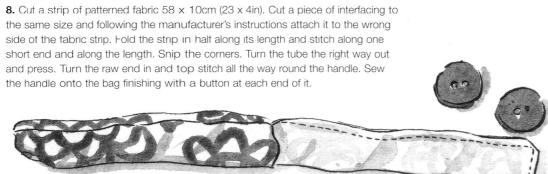

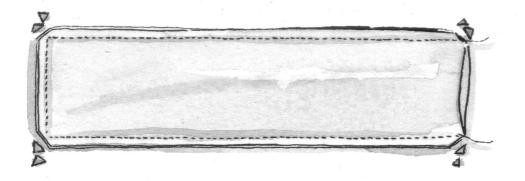

5. Cut two pieces of fabric 37 x 9cm (14½ x 3½in) for the strap using two different fabrics. Cut two pieces of interfacing to fit them and iron on following the manufacturer's instructions. With right sides together, pin and stitch along both long sides and one end. Snip the corners and turn the right way out and press.

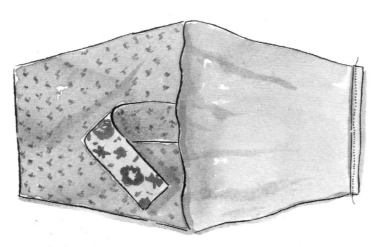

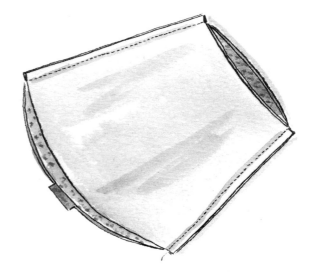

6. Again using the paper pattern, cut out two pieces of plain fabric for the lining. With right sides together, if applicable, pin and stitch together along both sides. Slip over the patchwork bag, lining up the top raw edges of both. Push the strap piece between the patchwork bag and lining at the back, leaving the raw end sticking out slightly. Pin and machine stitch all the way round the top.

7. Turn the right way out. Fold the bottom of the lining bag in by 1cm (½in) and machine stitch the bottom of the bag closed. Push the lining inside the bag.

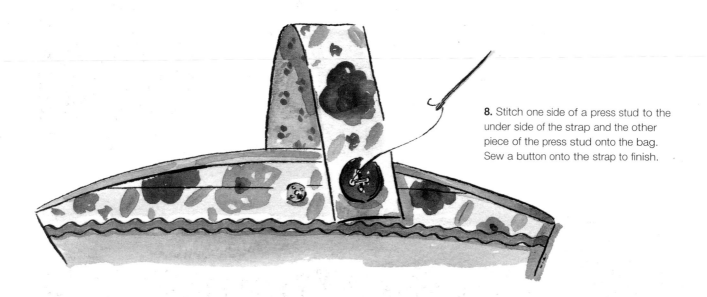

8. Stitch one side of a press stud to the under side of the strap and the other piece of the press stud onto the bag. Sew a button onto the strap to finish.

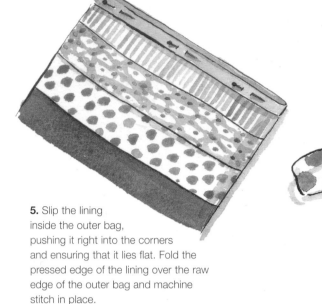

5. Slip the lining inside the outer bag, pushing it right into the corners and ensuring that it lies flat. Fold the pressed edge of the lining over the raw edge of the outer bag and machine stitch in place.

6. Measure and cut two pieces of fabric 7 x 82cm (2¾ x 32in). Iron interfacing to the back of both pieces following the manufacturer's instructions. With right sides together, pin and stitch along both long sides and one end. Snip the corners and turn the right way out. Turn the end in by 1cm (½in) and press. Hand stitch closed. Machine stitch this strap onto the bag 10cm (4in) from the right hand side on the back and 10cm (4in) from the left hand side on the front.

7. Take the strip from step 1 and cut so that it is seven panels of fabric long. Cut a rounded shape on each band of fabric to form a petal shape, either freehand or draw a shape onto paper and use as your pattern.

8. Make a running stitch along the bottom of the strip and pull the thread to gather it up to form the flower. Finish with a few small stitches and sew a button in the centre, sewing it onto the laundry bag securely.

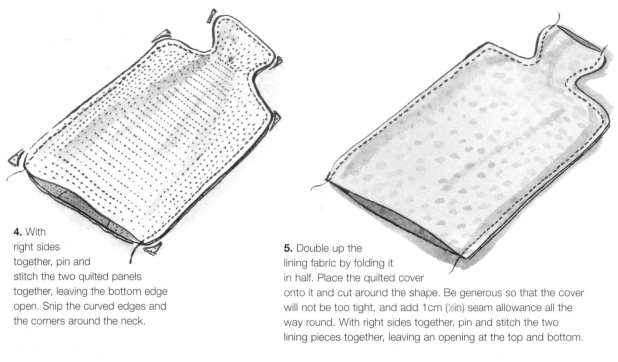

4. With
right sides
together, pin and
stitch the two quilted panels
together, leaving the bottom edge
open. Snip the curved edges and
the corners around the neck.

5. Double up the
lining fabric by folding it
in half. Place the quilted cover
onto it and cut around the shape. Be generous so that the cover
will not be too tight, and add 1cm (½in) seam allowance all the
way round. With right sides together, pin and stitch the two
lining pieces together, leaving an opening at the top and bottom.

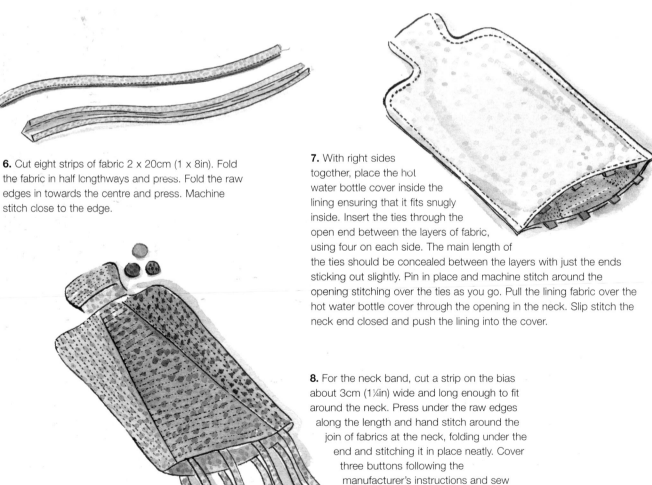

6. Cut eight strips of fabric 2 x 20cm (1 x 8in). Fold
the fabric in half lengthways and press. Fold the raw
edges in towards the centre and press. Machine
stitch close to the edge.

7. With right sides
together, place the hot
water bottle cover inside the
lining ensuring that it fits snugly
inside. Insert the ties through the
open end between the layers of fabric,
using four on each side. The main length of
the ties should be concealed between the layers with just the ends
sticking out slightly. Pin in place and machine stitch around the
opening stitching over the ties as you go. Pull the lining fabric over the
hot water bottle cover through the opening in the neck. Slip stitch the
neck end closed and push the lining into the cover.

8. For the neck band, cut a strip on the bias
about 3cm (1¼in) wide and long enough to fit
around the neck. Press under the raw edges
along the length and hand stitch around the
join of fabrics at the neck, folding under the
end and stitching it in place neatly. Cover
three buttons following the
manufacturer's instructions and sew
them onto the neck. Put the hot water
bottle inside the cover and tie the ties
into neat bows.

Green Handbag

The large green spot fabric used in this bag is one of my favourites and I have used it in several sewing projects. I only had small scraps left, which was the inspiration for this bag – I mixed it with other green fabrics to create a cute handbag. Edging the top of the bag with velvet ribbon adds a stylish trim, with a fabric rosette flower adding the finishing touch.

3 hours

MATERIALS

Scraps of fabric in shades of green for the patchwork
50 x 40cm (20 x 16in) fabric for the side gussets, back and base
60 x 40cm (24 x 16in) plain fabric for the lining
73.5 x 46cm (32 x 18½in) cotton wadding
40 x 15cm (16 x 6in) plain fabric
35 x 14cm (14 x 5½in) patterned fabric
80cm (32in) length of velvet ribbon
Button

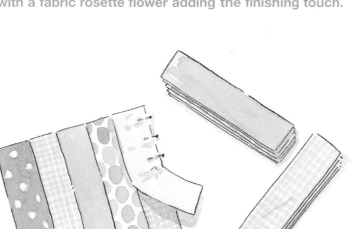

1. Measure and cut 15 strips of assorted pieces of green fabric 4.5 x 19cm (2 x 8in). Lay them out side by side and move them around until you are happy with the arrangement. With right sides together, pin and stitch them together with a 1cm (½in) seam, pressing the seams open as you go until all the strips are joined together.

2. Measure and cut a strip of fabric 39.5 x 5.5cm (16 x 2¼in) for the base. Cut two strips 19 x 5.5cm (8 x 2¼in) for the side gussets. With right sides together, pin and stitch each short piece to either end of the longer piece. Press all the seams open.

3. Measure and cut a piece of wadding 39.5 x 19cm (16 x 8in) and lay the patchwork panel right side up on to it. Cut a strip of wadding 73.5 x 5.5cm (32 x 2¼in). Lay this onto the wrong side of the gusset and base strip. Place this with right sides together onto the patchwork panel lining up the raw edges along one long side. Pin in place.

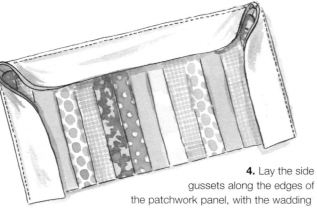

4. Lay the side gussets along the edges of the patchwork panel, with the wadding in place and pin and stitch in place. Make a snip at both corners in the seam allowance. Cut a rectangle of fabric and a panel of wadding both measuring 39.5 x 19cm (16 x 8in). With right sides together and with the wadding on the wrong side, pin and stitch the back of the bag onto the side gussets and base of the bag, again snipping the corners of the seam allowance.

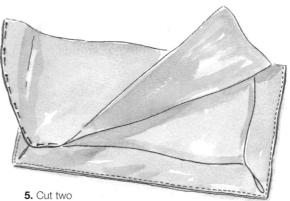

5. Cut two rectangles of lining fabric measuring 39.5 x 19cm (16 x 8in) and a side and base strip of lining fabric measuring 73.5 x 5.5cm (32 x 2½in). Stitch the long strip along both ends and one long side of one of the rectangles. Snip the corners. Stitch the remaining rectangle to the other side of the side and base strip to form the lining. Press.

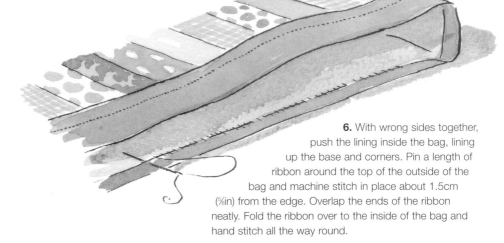

6. With wrong sides together, push the lining inside the bag, lining up the base and corners. Pin a length of ribbon around the top of the outside of the bag and machine stitch in place about 1.5cm (⅝in) from the edge. Overlap the ends of the ribbon neatly. Fold the ribbon over to the inside of the bag and hand stitch all the way round.

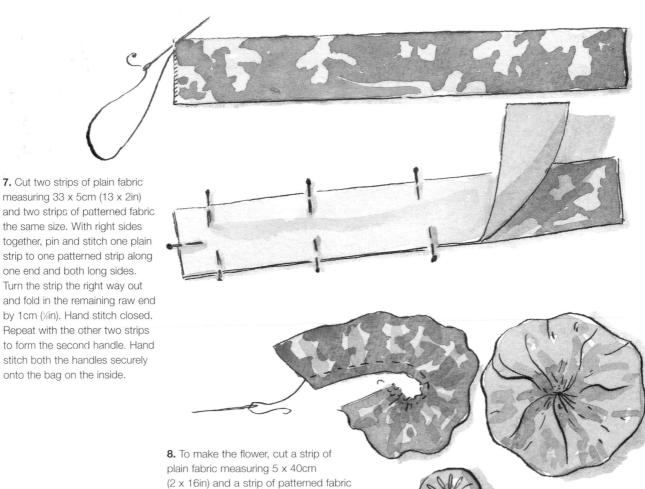

7. Cut two strips of plain fabric measuring 33 x 5cm (13 x 2in) and two strips of patterned fabric the same size. With right sides together, pin and stitch one plain strip to one patterned strip along one end and both long sides. Turn the strip the right way out and fold in the remaining raw end by 1cm (½in). Hand stitch closed. Repeat with the other two strips to form the second handle. Hand stitch both the handles securely onto the bag on the inside.

8. To make the flower, cut a strip of plain fabric measuring 5 x 40cm (2 x 16in) and a strip of patterned fabric 4 x 35cm (1½ x 14in). Make a running stitch along one long side of each of the strips and gather to form two rosette shapes. Hand stitch them together with a button in the middle and sew the flower onto the bag securely.

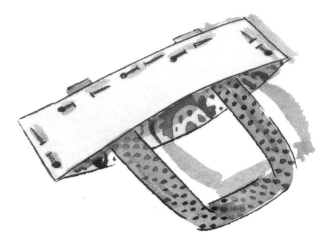

5. To make the band across the top of the bag, measure and cut four 8 x 32cm (3 x 12½in) rectangles. Again iron interfacing to the back of them. With right sides together, pin around three sides to join two of them together. Insert the ends of one of the handles between the two layers so that the ends stick out slightly through the seam. Stitch in place. Repeat with the other two pieces and the other handle.

6. Make a running stitch along each side of the patchwork bag and gather it up so that it will fit exactly inside the top band. With right sides together, pin and stitch the gathered edge of the bag to the outer side of the top bar on both sides of the bag.

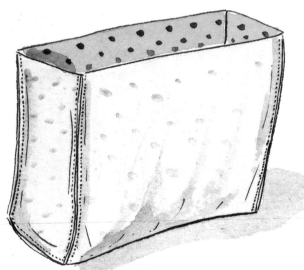

7. Measure and cut one 59 x 41cm (23 x 16in) rectangle of lining fabric and two 12 x 25cm (4¾ x 10in) rectangles. In the same way as the outer bag, with right sides together, pin and stitch the side gussets to the main fabric again starting and finishing the stitching 1cm (½in) from the top edge to form a bag. Press the seams open and snip the corners.

8. Slip the lining bag over the outer bag with right sides together. Pin and stitch across the top of the gussets. Turn the lining the right way out and push into the bag. Make a running stitch across the top of both sides of the lining fabric so that it is the same width as the outer bag. Turn under 1cm (½in) to the wrong side on the top bands and pin and hand stitch in place along the lining. Press.

Picnic Blanket

This lovely vintage-style picnic blanket is made from an old floral tablecloth that was stained in places and could no longer be used. Squares of this have been joined with plain pink fabric to make the main panel, which has been edged with gingham and trimmed with a contrasting ribbon and buttons. Use heavy-weight wadding and a cotton fabric backing to make a hardy blanket that will make your picnic as comfortable and enjoyable as can be.

2 hours

MATERIALS

100 x 50cm (40 x 20in) of plain fabric

90 x 50cm (36 x 20in) of floral fabric

90 x 50cm (36 x 20in) piece of gingham fabric

102cm (41in) square of spotty fabric for the backing

100cm (40in) square of cotton wadding

375cm (148in) length of ribbon

4 buttons

1. Cut a paper square measuring 21cm (8½in). Use this to cut out eight squares of plain fabric and eight squares of floral fabric. Lay them alternately in a block of four squares by four. With right sides together, pin and stitch the squares together in strips with a 5mm (¼in) seam to form four strips. Press the seams open.

2. With right sides together, pin and stitch the strips together with a 5mm (¼in) seam in the correct order to form a chequerboard pattern. Press seams open.

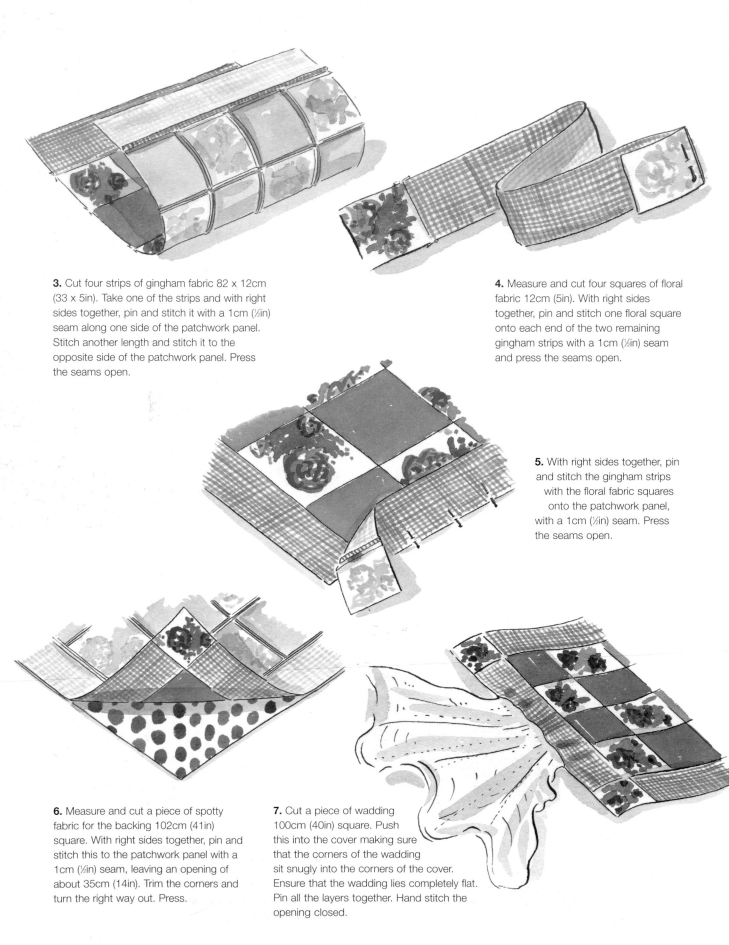

3. Cut four strips of gingham fabric 82 x 12cm (33 x 5in). Take one of the strips and with right sides together, pin and stitch it with a 1cm (½in) seam along one side of the patchwork panel. Stitch another length and stitch it to the opposite side of the patchwork panel. Press the seams open.

4. Measure and cut four squares of floral fabric 12cm (5in). With right sides together, pin and stitch one floral square onto each end of the two remaining gingham strips with a 1cm (½in) seam and press the seams open.

5. With right sides together, pin and stitch the gingham strips with the floral fabric squares onto the patchwork panel, with a 1cm (½in) seam. Press the seams open.

6. Measure and cut a piece of spotty fabric for the backing 102cm (41in) square. With right sides together, pin and stitch this to the patchwork panel with a 1cm (½in) seam, leaving an opening of about 35cm (14in). Trim the corners and turn the right way out. Press.

7. Cut a piece of wadding 100cm (40in) square. Push this into the cover making sure that the corners of the wadding sit snugly into the corners of the cover. Ensure that the wadding lies completely flat. Pin all the layers together. Hand stitch the opening closed.

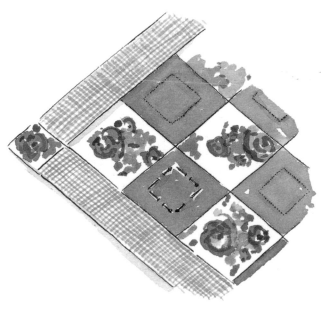

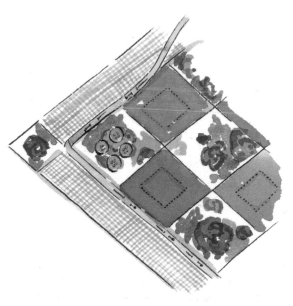

8. Marking the position with pins (or masking tape if you find that easier), measure a square on each of the plain patchwork squares and machine stitch through all layers.

9. Pin and stitch ribbon along the edge of the border to cover the join, folding the ribbon neatly at the corners and stitching along both edges of it. Finish with a button sewn onto each corner of the ribbon.

Beach Bag

This beach bag is most definitely as practical as it is good looking. Made from hard-wearing natural linen, it has handy pockets for sunglasses, phone and other essentials on one side, a large pocket on the other side perfect for holding a Frisbee, and enough room inside to hold everything you will need for a fun day at the seaside. Metal eyelets are available from haberdashery stores and give a smart professional finish when combined with thick rope used as handles, perfectly in keeping with the seaside theme.

4 hours

MATERIALS

50 x 105cm (20 x 42in) piece of upholstery-weight linen

50 x 80cm (20 x 32in) piece of fabric for lining

35 x 50cm (14 x 20in) pieces of four different fabrics for pockets

4 eyelets

Eyelet machine

120cm (48in) length of rope for handles

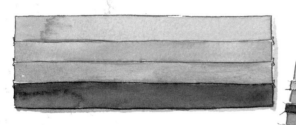

1. To make the pockets, cut a strip from each of the four co-ordinating fabrics measuring 80 x 7cm (32 x 2½in). With right sides together, pin and stitch the strips together along the long edges and press the seams open. Cut a piece 32cm (12½in) long by the depth of the strip for the Frisbee pocket. Cut a piece 18cm (7in) long for the flat pocket and a piece 26cm (10¼in) long for the folded pocket. To create the seam covers, cut strips of three of the fabrics 2.5cm (1in) wide by the widths of the two smaller pockets. Fold the raw edges in towards the centre by 5mm (¼in) and press. Place these strips over the seams of the pocket fronts and top stitch them in place.

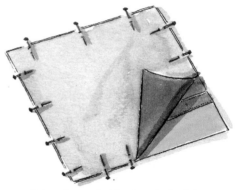

2. Lay the pocket fronts onto the lining fabric and cut out a piece of lining for each. Place each pocket front right sides together with its lining piece and stitch all the way round, leaving a small opening. Snip off the corners and turn the pocket right way out. Press. Repeat for all three pockets.

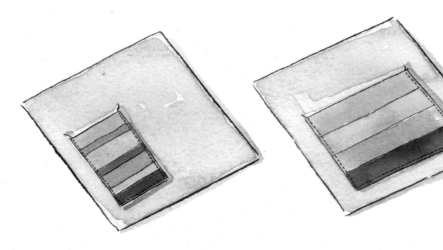

3. Cut out two pieces of linen each 49cm (19¼in) square. Lay these onto the work surface right sides up. Place the flat pocket about 14cm (5½in) from the top and pin and stitch in place around three sides, leaving an opening at the top and stitching a few millimetres from the edge. Repeat this with the Frisbee pocket on the second linen square.

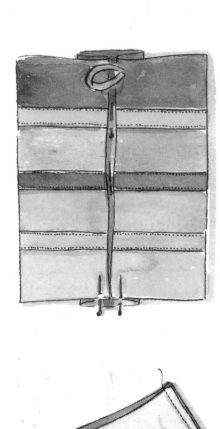

4. Take the folded pocket piece and mark the centre with pins. Make a fold approximately 1.5cm (⅝in) deep, bring it towards the centre mark and pin in place at the base. Repeat at the other side. Using a scrap of fabric cut a strip 8 x 2.5cm (3 x 1in). Press in half lengthways, open out and press in raw edges to the centre fold. Machine stitch close to the edge. Make it into a loop and hand stitch it onto one side of the pocket pleat. Position this pocket onto the bag front and stitch in place along three sides. Sew a button onto the other side of the pocket so you can fit the loop over it.

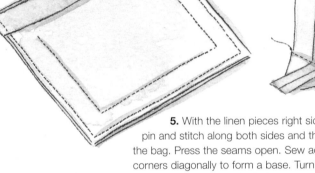

5. With the linen pieces right sides together, pin and stitch along both sides and the bottom of the bag. Press the seams open. Sew across the corners diagonally to form a base. Turn top over to the wrong side by 7.5cm (3in) to create a yoke and press along the folded edge. Turn the bag right side out and open out the yoke again.

6. Cut two rectangles of fabric 49 x 40cm (19¼ x 15¾in) for the lining. With right sides together, pin and stitch along the two shorter sides and across the bottom and press the seams open. As with the main bag pieces, sew diagonally across the corners to create a base.

7. To join the lining to the bag, slip the lining over the linen bag with right sides together. Match the side seams and pin in place. At the top edge, align the raw edges of the yoke on the main fabric and the lining and machine stitch around them leaving an opening of about 12cm (5in). Remove the pins at the sides and then turn the lining right side out through the opening and push it into the bag. Hand stitch the opening closed.

8. Mark the position for the eyelets on the front and the back of the bag, about 15cm (6in) in from each outer edge. Following the manufacturer's instructions, fix the eyelets in place. Thread a length of rope around 60cm (24in) long through two eyelets and tie the ends into knots. Repeat through the other two eyelets.

Bunting

When making sewing projects, there are inevitably lots of oddments of fabric left over. Bunting is a quick and easy way of using up these scraps to create a cute decoration for just about anywhere in the home. Mix colours and patterns using different fabrics on each side of each triangle, finishing the bunting with simple flower and button embellishments and stitching them onto ribbon.

1 hour

MATERIALS

Scraps of fabrics at least 25 x 27cm (10 x 11in)

Paper for pattern

Buttons

Ribbon

1. Using the template on page 168, cut out a paper pattern. Decide how many bunting triangles you would like and cut two fabric triangles for each one. With right sides together, pin and stitch two fabric triangles together, starting and finishing the stitches 2cm (⅞in) from the top edge.

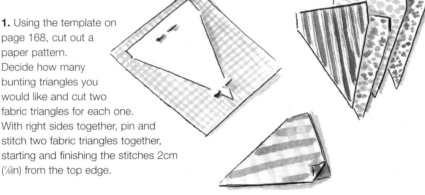

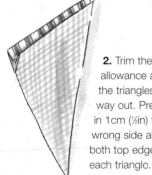

2. Trim the seam allowance and turn the triangles the right way out. Press. Turn in 1cm (½in) to the wrong side along both top edges of each triangle.

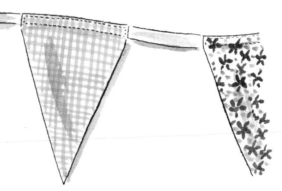

3. Slip the ribbon between the top opening of the triangles, and pin and stitch in place with a double row of stitches.

4. Using the templates on page 168, cut out a large and a small flower shape from paper and use them to cut out a large and small fabric flower for each triangle. Hand stitch the flowers onto the triangles, sewing a button in the middle of each.

Purse

A very simple patchwork project has been enhanced with simple embroidery stitches (see the techniques section for these stitches) to make this sweet purse with a shop-bought (or home made if you crochet as well as sew!) flower to decorate it. The purse has been lined with pretty fabric and could easily be made on a larger scale and used as a clutch bag – or a shoulder bag if a strap is attached.

MATERIALS

35 x 20cm (14 x 8in) of each of three plain coloured linens

25 x 35cm (10 x 14in) piece of fabric for the lining

Embroidery thread in three colours and needle

Crochet flower

Press stud

3 hours

1. Measure and cut four strips of linen 6 x 30cm (2¼ x 12in). With right sides together, pin and stitch them together. Press the seams open.

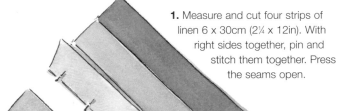

2. Following the instructions on the techniques pages, embroider a fly stitch along the outer joins of the patchwork strips, a cross-stitch along another one and a zigzag stitch along the remaining one.

3. Measure and cut a rectangle 22 x 30cm (8 x 12in) from the lining fabric. With right sides together, pin and stitch the patchwork panel to the lining fabric, leaving an opening of about 5cm (2in) along one side. Snip the corners off and turn the right way out. Press and hand stitch the opening closed.

4. Fold the fabric over by 10cm (4in) and stitch down both sides. Stitch one side of the press stud to the middle of the purse, near the top edge and the other half to the underside of the flap. Stitch a flower onto the purse to decorate it.

Techniques

Basic equipment

Most of the equipment that is needed for quilting will probably already be part of your sewing kit. Specific tools are listed under the Materials list for each project but here are the 'basics' that you will need throughout this book:

Sewing machine

A sewing machine is essential, although a basic model is all that is required. It is advisable to replace the needles regularly, especially when quilting, to keep them nice and sharp. Special quilting needles are available and are good for stitching through thick layers.

Scissors

You will need a pair of large shears for cutting fabrics – which need to be kept really sharp – a pair of small embroidery scissors for cutting seam allowances and snipping threads, and a pair of good craft scissors for cutting patterns.

Rotary cutter and mat

This tool allows you to cut through several layers very accurately and saves a lot of time if you have lots of patchwork pieces to cut. The blade needs to be kept very sharp and must be handled with care. A self-healing mat provides an ideal surface for cutting. Rotary rulers are available but a standard acrylic ruler will be fine. A set square can also be useful.

Rotary cutter

Pins

Long, sharp pins will be needed and safety pins can be useful for keeping layers of quilting together while working on them. Special quilter's pins are available that have a flat head, which can be useful for machine quilting.

Iron

This is essential for quilting and is used throughout all the projects here. Pressing seams open creates a neat professional finish and makes sewing patchwork much easier.

Dressmaker's chalk pencil

This is needed for making temporary marks on fabric to mark stitching lines and can be brushed off easily.

Pattern paper

This paper is marked with equally spaced horizontal and vertical lines and is used to make pattern pieces.

Fabrics

Fabrics should be pre-washed and ironed when making patchwork and quilting. When piecing small patches of fabric together it can be useful to spray a little starch onto the fabric to make it slightly stiffer. Generally, it is a good idea to use fabrics of a similar weight in a project, with cotton and linen fabrics being the easiest to handle. The colours used are important as lighter and darker tones can change the look and focus of patchwork and different colours and patterns can create very different effects. Plain fabrics and stripes are useful for backing quilts.

Wadding

There is a selection of this available from fabric and quilting shops in a variety of widths and thickness. Cotton wadding is the most expensive and is often not washable (consult the manufacturer's instructions) but it drapes beautifully and gives a lovely soft finish. Polyester wadding is the cheaper option, is machine washable and gives a slightly stiffer finish. As with fabrics, it is advisable to wash the wadding before using it.

Templates

To make a template for a fabric shape, enlarge or reduce it on a photocopier to the required size. If you are cutting out with scissors, simply cut out the photocopied shape and pin it to the fabric to use as a pattern piece. If you are using a rotary cutter to cut your fabric you will need to make a card template. Trace the motif onto tracing paper. Turn the tracing paper over and scribble over the drawn lines with a pencil. Turn the tracing paper over again and place on a piece of card. Draw over the lines and the shape will be transferred to the card. Cut the shape out and use as your pattern piece.

Piecing

This means joining pieces of fabric together to form larger panels. I have generally used a seam allowance of 1cm (½in) throughout this book, which means that you stitch exactly 1cm (½in) from the raw edge. Use the stitching guide on your sewing machine if there is one, or measure from the machine needle and stick a piece of masking tape onto the stitching plate to use as your guide.

When piecing lots of shapes (for a quilt, say) stitch them in a chain and then cut the threads, which speeds things up and saves thread too.

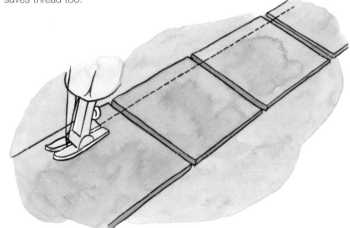

Chain piecing

Quilting

There are several ways to hold the layers of patchwork together to quilt them. Machine quilting is a quick and easy way to do this and is effective on large quilted projects. To stitch straight lines, masking tape can be stuck onto the surface of the fabric to act as a guide for the stitching, or dressmaker's chalk can be used. Ditch quilting is when the quilt is stitched along the seams of patchwork, making the stitches virtually invisible. Contour quilting is when the quilt is stitched within the patchwork, creating a slightly raised effect.

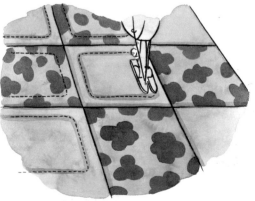

Contour quilting

Templates

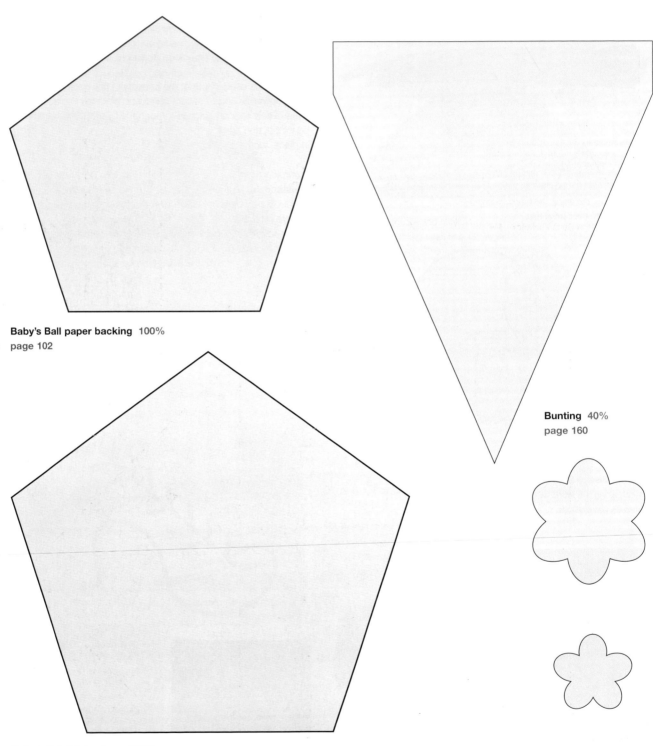

Baby's Ball paper backing 100%
page 102

Bunting 40%
page 160

Baby's Ball fabric piece 100%
page 102

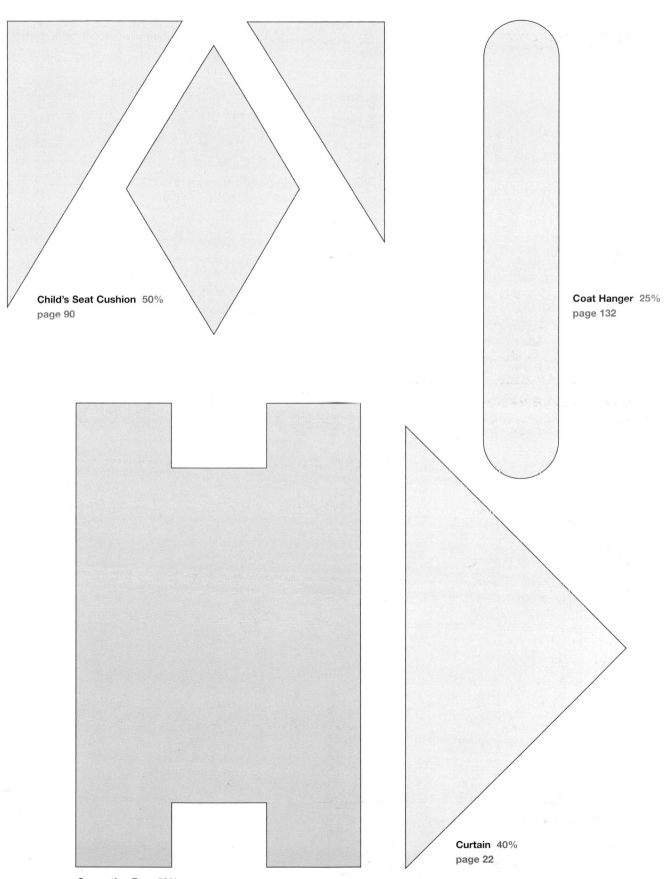

Child's Seat Cushion 50%
page 90

Coat Hanger 25%
page 132

Cosmetics Bag 50%
page 138

Curtain 40%
page 22

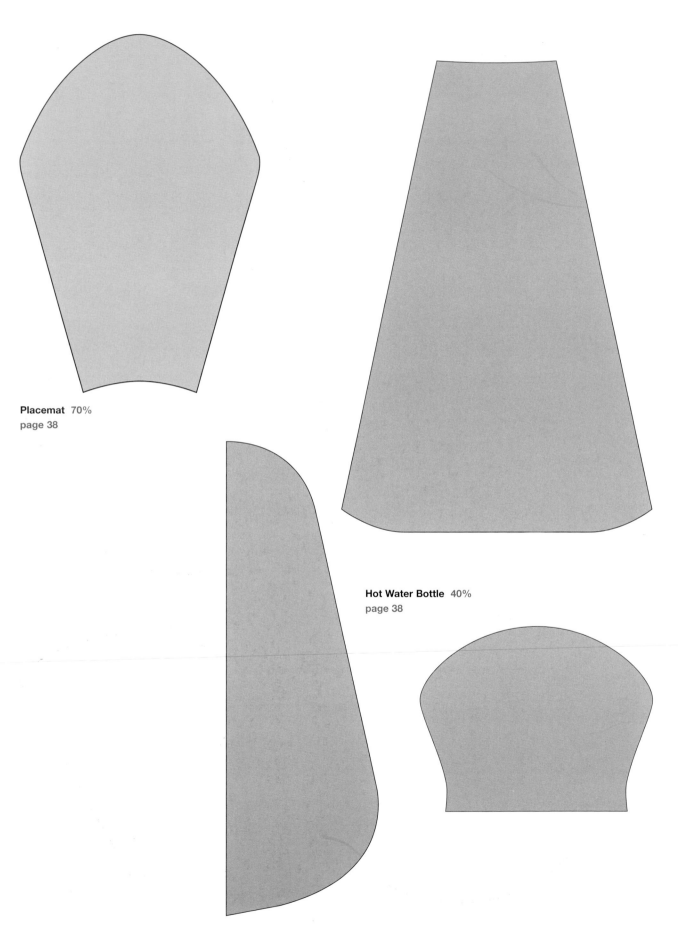

Placemat 70%
page 38

Hot Water Bottle 40%
page 38

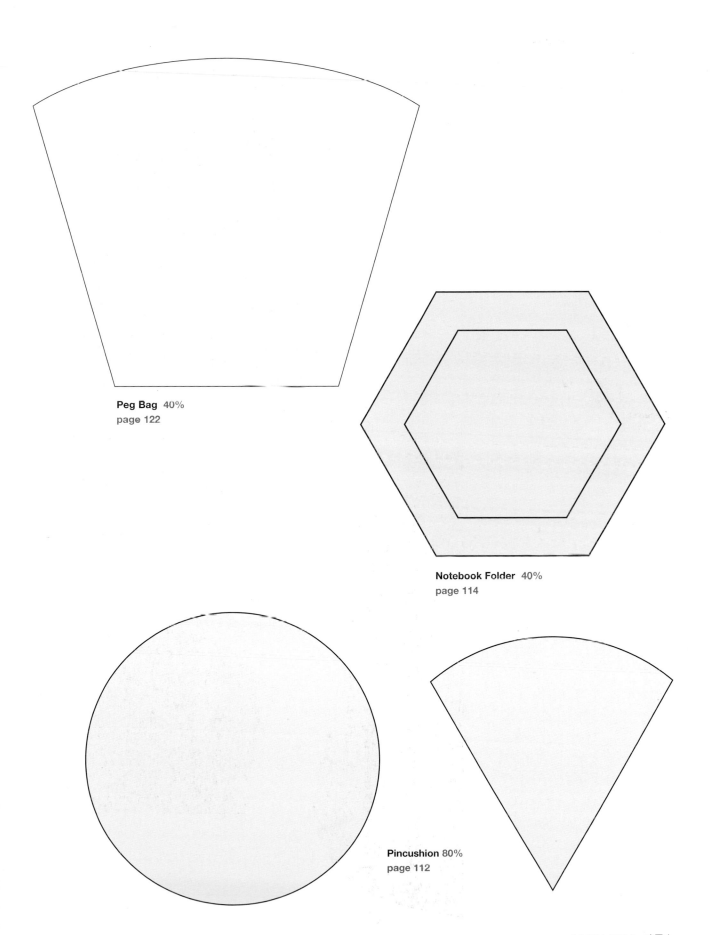

Peg Bag 40%
page 122

Notebook Folder 40%
page 114

Pincushion 80%
page 112

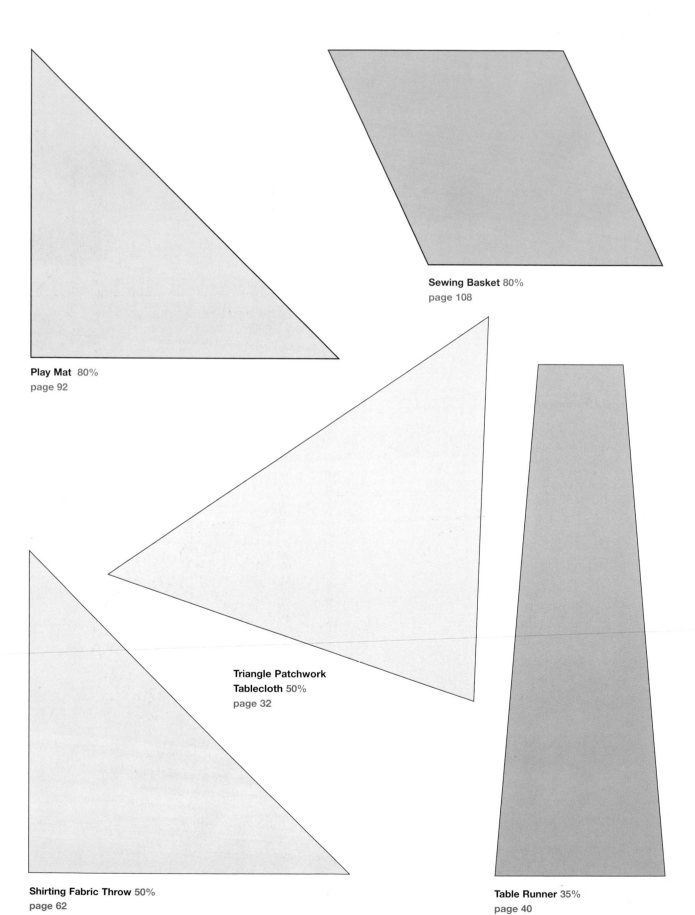

Sewing Basket 80%
page 108

Play Mat 80%
page 92

**Triangle Patchwork
Tablecloth** 50%
page 32

Shirting Fabric Throw 50%
page 62

Table Runner 35%
page 40

Tea Cosy 50%
page 44

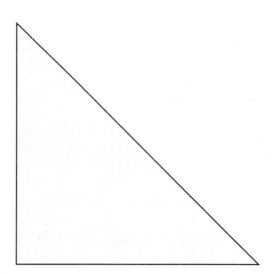

Bordered Towel 80%
page 140

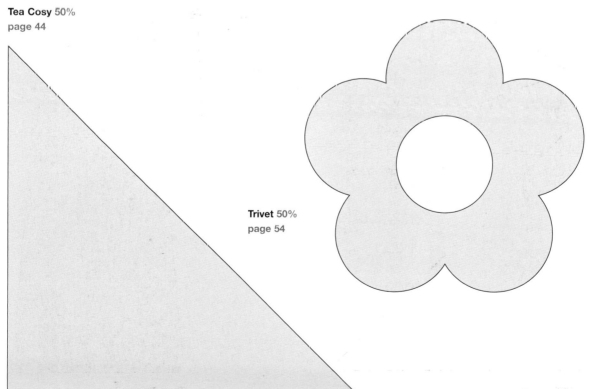

Trivet 50%
page 54

Suppliers

The Button Queen
19 Marylebone Lane
London W1V 2NF
020 7935 1505
www.thebuttonqueen.co.uk

Cath Kidston
08450 262 440
www.cathkidston.co.uk

The Cloth House
47 Berwick Street
London W1F 8SJ
020 7437 5155
www.clothhouse.com

Fabrics Galore
52–54 Lavender Hill
London SW11 5RH
020 7738 9589

Ian Mankin
109 Regent's Park Road
London NW1 8UR
020 7722 0997
www.ianmankin.com

Laura Ashley
0871 230 2301
www.lauraashley.com

John Lewis
Oxford Street
London W1A 1EX
020 7629 7711
www.johnlewis.com

Liberty
Regent Street
London W1B 5AH
020 7734 1234
www.liberty.co.uk

The Little Fabric Shop
www.littlefabric.com

The Quilt Room
20 West Street
Dorking
Surrey RH4 1BL
01306 740439
www.quiltroom.co.uk

Tikki Patchwork
293 Sandycombe Road
Kew
Surrey TW9 3LU
020 8948 8462
www.tikkilondon.com

VV Rouleaux
102 Marylebone Lane
London W1U 2QD
020 7224 5179
www.vvrouleaux.com

Amy Butler
www.amybutler.com

Britex Fabrics
146 Geary Street
San Francisco
CA 94108
415-392-2910
www.britexfabrics.com

Cia's Palette
4155 Grand Ave S
Minneapolis
MN 55409
612-229-5227
www.ciaspalette.com

Purl Patchwork
147 Sullivan Street
New York
NY 10012
212-420-8798
www.purlsoho.com

Reprodepot Fabrics
413-527-4047
www.reprodepot.com

Tinsel Trading Company
47 West 38th Street
New York
NY 10018
212-730-1030
www.tinseltrading.com

Z and S Fabrics
681 S. Muddy Creek Road
Denver
PA 17157
717-336-4026
www.zandsfabrics.com

Index

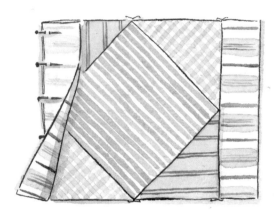

Acknowledgements

A big thank you to Debbie Patterson for the beautiful photography as ever,
and for boundless enthusiasm and good humour throughout
the project.

Thank you Michael Hill for the beautiful illustrations and being such a pleasure
to work with. Thank you to Marie Clayton for editing the book with such
attention to detail and to Pete Jorgensen and Sally Powell at Cico for all your
unstinting help and support. Many thanks to Cindy Richards for trusting me
to do this book in the first place.

A big thank you to Beverlee Regan, for designing and making the beach bag,
hot water bottle cover and cosmetics bag so beautifully. Thank you to Sandesh
Brown, for your very good taste in wool. A huge thank you to Gracie and Betty
for all your enthusiasm and encouragement and for many, many helpful
suggestions and ideas. And of course, thank you to Laurie Dahl for endless
amounts of patience and constant reassurances that I would meet my
deadlines. You were right, although it was a close call at times!